CULTURES OF THE WORLD
Albania

Cavendish
Square
New York

Published in 2021 by Cavendish Square Publishing, LLC
243 5th Avenue, Suite 136, New York, NY 10016

Website: cavendishsq.com

This publication represents the opinions and views of the author based on his or her personal experience, knowledge, and research. The information in this book serves as a general guide only. The author and publisher have used their best efforts in preparing this book and disclaim liability rising directly or indirectly from the use and application of this book.

All websites were available and accurate when this book was sent to press.

Library of Congress Cataloging-in-Publication Data

Names: Knowlton, MaryLee, 1946- author. | Nevins, Debbie, author.
Title: Albania / MaryLee Knowlton, Debbie Nevins.
Description: Third edition. | New York, NY : Cavendish Square Publishing, 2021. | Series: Cultures of the world | Includes bibliographical references and index.
Identifiers: LCCN 2020007822 (print) | LCCN 2020007823 (ebook) | ISBN 9781502655851 (library binding) | ISBN 9781502655868 (ebook)
Subjects: LCSH: Albania--Juvenile literature.
Classification: LCC DR910 .K6 2021 (print) | LCC DR910 (ebook) | DDC 949.65--dc23
LC record available at https://lccn.loc.gov/2020007822
LC ebook record available at https://lccn.loc.gov/2020007823

Editor, third edition: Debbie Nevins
Designer, third edition: Jessica Nevins

The photographs in this book are used by permission and through the courtesy of: Cover Marco Alhelm/Shutterstock.com; p. 1 nicolasdecorte/Shutterstock.com; pp. 3, 21 Ppictures/Shutterstock.com; p. 5 Ungvari Attila/Shutterstock.com; p. 6 Mitzo/Shutterstock.com; pp. 8, 38, 46, 56 GENT SHKULLAKU/AFP/Getty Images; p. 10 Zbigniew Dziok/Shutterstock.com; p. 12 pavalena/Shutterstock.com; p. 13 leszczem/Shutterstock.com; p. 16 Zbigniew Dziok/Shutterstock.com; p. 17 agrofruti/Shutterstock.com; p. 18 Szymon Mucha/Shutterstock.com; p. 19 Alla Simacheva/Shutterstock.com; p. 20 Ajdin Kamber/Shutterstock.com; p. 23 Jess Kraft/Shutterstock.com; p. 24 PaulSat/Shutterstock.com; p. 27 S-F/Shutterstock.com; p. 29 CCat82/Shutterstock.com; p. 31 © CORBIS/Corbis via Getty Images; p. 33 ullstein bild/ullstein bild via Getty Images; p. 35 Georges MERILLON/Gamma-Rapho via Getty Images; p. 36 Larry Downing/Sygma/Sygma via Getty Images; p. 37 Sion Touhig/Sygma/Sygma via Getty Images; p. 40 msnobody/Shutterstock.com; p. 42 Restimage/Shutterstock.com; p. 44 Leonid Andronov/Shutterstock.com; p. 45 roibu/Shutterstock.com; p. 48 826A IA/Shutterstock.com; p. 54 Uwe Seidner/Shutterstock.com; p. 58 Michal Ninger/Shutterstock.com; pp. 60, 72, 112, 130, 131 A Daily Odyssey/Shutterstock.com; p. 62 Aldo91/Shutterstock.com; pp. 63, 104 ollirg/Shutterstock.com; p. 64 Daniel Reiner/Shutterstock.com; p. 66 MehmetO/Shutterstock.com; p. 67 marketa1982/Shutterstock.com; p. 68 Katsiuba Volha/Shutterstock.com; p. 70 Northfoto/Shutterstock.com; p. 75 Bas van den Heuvel/Shutterstock.com; p. 76 Maria Studio/Shutterstock.com; p. 78 Andrea Seemann/Shutterstock.com; pp. 82, 100 Zvonimir Atletic/Shutterstock.com; p. 84 Denis Kabanov/Shutterstock.com; p. 87 RussieseO/Shutterstock.com; pp. 88, 110 marketa1982/Shutterstock.com; p. 90 Wolfgang Kaehler/LightRocket via Getty Images; p. 93 Uta Scholl/Shutterstock.com; p. 96 Aleksandar Todorovic/Shutterstock.com; p. 98 Leonardo Cendamo/Getty Images; p. 103 Brilliant Eye/Shutterstock.com; p. 105 (top) milosk50/Shutterstock.com; p. 105 (bottom) posztos/Shutterstock.com; p. 106 Alla Simacheva/Shutterstock.com; p. 108 smart.art/Shutterstock.com; p. 111 Laszlo Szirtesi/Shutterstock.com; p. 113 igli Ilubani/Shutterstock.com; p. 115 zefart/Shutterstock.com; p. 116 Daniel Reiner/Shutterstock.com; p. 118 Edvin Rushitaj/Shutterstock.com; p. 121 Teresa Otto/Shutterstock.com; p. 122 SHV_photo/Shutterstock.com; p. 124 Tomasz Wozniak/Shutterstock.com; p. 126 Fredy Thuerig/Shutterstock.com; p. 127 Ipek Morel/Shutterstock.com; p. 128 Fanfo/Shutterstock.com.

Some of the images in this book illustrate individuals who are models. The depictions do not imply actual situations or events.

CPSIA compliance information: Batch #CS20CSQ: For further information contact Cavendish Square Publishing LLC, New York, New York, at 1-877-980-4450.

Printed in the United States of America

Find us on

CONTENTS

ALBANIA TODAY

ALBANIA TODAY IS AT A CROSSROADS. IT'S AN EMERGING democracy struggling to adjust to a world it was shut off from for nearly 50 years. During that time, from about 1944 to 1992, Albania was like the North Korea of Europe—a closed, communist, hermit nation under the complete control of one cruel, self-obsessed leader. Cut off from the capitalist West as well as from the communist East, Albania became one of the poorest and most isolated countries in Europe. Albania is now trying to put that past behind it and take its place as a modern European country, but as it strives, powerful forces are pulling it in other directions.

Where is Albania? Many people in the West might find it difficult to place among the better-known nations of Europe. When the country was closed off for all those years, it was, perhaps, easy for the outside world to forget it even existed. Its neighbors were making far more noise—and news—in those years, and indeed, right up through the end of the 20th century.

Also, Albania is rather small for a country, at least compared to the likes of France or Germany. In area, it's slightly larger than Massachusetts and just a bit smaller than Maryland. It's located in south-central Europe in a region often called the Balkans. From

The Buna River, also known as the Bojana, flows through the Albanian countryside.

Italy, Albania is just a hop over the Adriatic Sea. It has a 225-mile (362-kilometer) coastline on that same body of water. To its south lies Greece, and its other neighbors in the Balkan region are some of the nations that comprised the communist country of Yugoslavia for much of the 20th century.

Albania may be small, but its history and geography place it in many of the biggest stories of the past. Until the 20th century, it had never had a national government of its own, having been dominated by a series of empires—Roman, Greek, Byzantine, and Ottoman. Through all of these subjugations, including the most recent under communism, the Albanian people maintained their identity, both within and beyond the country's borders.

The Balkan region is a part of the world where "East meets West"— where the religions and cultures of Europe collide with those of Western

Asia and the former Ottoman Empire. Christianity meets Islam, and within Christianity itself, the Roman Catholic Church encounters the Eastern Orthodox faith. This is evident in Albania, where a little more than half the people are Muslim and just less than one fifth are Christian—and those Christians are divided between Roman Catholics and Eastern Orthodox. However, for all Albanians, religion is as much a matter of culture and identity as it is of faith. This is because they were banned from practicing any religion at all for half a century under the communist government. Today, Albanians are finding their way back to the lost customs of their ancestors, while at the same time catching up with modernity and building a cohesive identity as a people and a nation.

When longtime Albanian dictator Enver Hoxha (enn-VEHR HAW-dja) died in 1985, he left behind a power vacuum. Although he had chosen a successor, the new government's iron fist was simply not strong enough to hold back inevitable change. Albanians wanted to transform their country into a democratic nation. That couldn't happen overnight, though, and in any event, the politicians didn't quite know how to bring this change about. Therefore, as often happens in times of political instability, heavily muscled organized crime and its loyal companion, corruption, came rushing into the void. They ushered in a period of predatory capitalism and fraudulent financial schemes that kept Albania impoverished, unsettled, and unsafe.

Meanwhile, next door, Marshal Tito, the communist strongman who had been holding Yugoslavia together for decades, died as well. By the start of the 1990s, in a sort of "perfect storm," the world's communist superpower, the Soviet Union, broke apart, and just like dominoes, communist regimes fell throughout the countries of Eastern Europe too. It was a heady time, but a dangerous one. Communist Yugoslavia split apart, but as it did, its constituent states became involved in an intense series of wars. Albania was struggling with its own newfound freedom, and it couldn't help but be impacted by the violence.

In the 21st century, following the turmoil of the 1990s, Albania has been working on integrating into Europe. It joined the North Atlantic Treaty Organization, or NATO, a mutual defense alliance of 29 member countries

In 2008, a banner in Mother Teresa Square in Tirana celebrates the country's invitation to join NATO. The banner reads, "Albania in NATO." Albania did not officially join until the following year.

from North America and Europe, in 2009. Formed in 1949 in opposition to communism and the Soviet Union, NATO has since expanded to include several formerly communist nations, including Albania.

In a similar way, Albania would like to join the European Union (EU), a political and economic organization of 27 European member nations. To do so, a country must have a stable democratic government, operate under the rule of law with respect for human rights and minorities, and have a functioning market economy. In other words, Albania must prove that it is a successful democratic nation with a resilient free-market economy. That's a big leap for Albania, and as of early 2020, it has not yet passed the test.

Corruption still reigns, though the government has been trying to address it. Unfortunately, it is the government itself that is accused of corruption. Also, the country's illegal drug trade—the domain of organized crime—is said to be the largest sector of Albania's economy, if not an officially recognized one.

Adding to the problems for Albania (and its neighbor North Macedonia, which is in a similar situation in regard to the EU) is Europe itself. The continent's own economic woes, coupled with rising ultranationalist extremism and complicated by rising aggression from Russia—as demonstrated by its theft in 2014 of Ukraine's Crimean peninsula (with no substantive response from Europe)—are all daunting indications of a possibly weakening Europe. Just as the EU blocked further membership negotiations for Albania and North Macedonia in October 2019, it was simultaneously preparing to lose one of its biggest players. The United Kingdom left the EU on January 31, 2020, leaving aspiring nations to wonder: Is the EU strong enough to last?

In a 2018 survey, 95 percent of Albanians said they believed EU membership would benefit the country. The country's prime minister, Edi Rama, said joining the EU was about "finally having the possibility to place ourselves in a safe zone from the curse of history." However, he warned that if Europe turns its back on Albania, Islamist radicals or powerful interests from Russia and China would fill the void.

So far, however, the small country on the Adriatic endeavors toward its goals. It's trying to attract tourists and foreign business investment. It has a lot to offer—from spectacular, unspoiled alpine mountains, to ancient castles and historic cities, to beautiful beaches on the "Albanian Riviera." The mix of cultures, East and West, makes it a special place. Will Albania succeed in becoming the best it can be, or will it fall to powerful, dangerous forces? Albania's story is ready for its next chapter.

GEOGRAPHY

Sunlight can barely find its way between the cliffs of the extremely narrow Lengarica Canyon, a dramatic part of the Fir of Hotove–Dangelli National Park in southern Albania.

1

ALBANIA IS A SMALL COUNTRY. With an area of 11,010 square miles (28,748 square kilometers), it's a bit larger than the state of Massachusetts. It's located on the southeastern coast of the Adriatic Sea, just across from the heel of the boot of Italy. Its position on the western side of the Balkan Peninsula is of great political significance, and in geographical terms makes it a Mediterranean country with distinct seasons and a rich variety of plants and animals.

Albania borders Montenegro to the northwest, Kosovo to the northeast, North Macedonia to the east, and Greece to the south. The Adriatic Sea and the Ionian Sea form its western and southwestern borders.

Albania's land is mostly hills and mountains, many of them covered with forests. Mount Korab (sometimes called Golem Korab) is the highest mountain at 9,068 feet (2,764 meters). Coastal plains account for about 20 percent of the land.

This map shows Albania and its major cities, along with its neighboring countries.

GEOGRAPHICAL REGIONS

Albania has four main geographical regions.

WESTERN LOWLANDS   This predominantly flat land area follows the coastline for about 125 miles (200 km) and extends inland about 30 miles (50 km). It varies from sandy beaches on the shore to inland rivers and lakes surrounded by rich farmland. Albania's Adriatic coastline has many bays with clear water and fine sand; its largest cities are Durres and Vlore. The widest part of the lowlands is dominated by the Plain of Myzeqe, a once-swampy area that has been partially reclaimed as farmland. The lowlands are surrounded by mountains to the north, east, and south.

NORTHERN MOUNTAIN REGION   Defined by the Albanian Alps, an extension of the Dinaric Alps, this is the most rugged part of the country. In fact, the Albanian Alps, or Prokletije, are also sometimes called the Accursed Mountains. The region is characterized by its cold climate, rich vegetation, deep valleys, numerous rivers, glacial lakes, and jutting, pyramid-shaped peaks. Maja Jezerce, the highest peak in the Dinaric Alps at 8,839 feet (2,694 m), is the second-highest peak in Albania. The region has spectacular scenery, but the rough terrain has kept it sparsely populated.

CENTRAL MOUNTAIN REGION   This area is dominated by three mountain ranges, each running roughly parallel to the eastern border of Albania. The country's highest mountain, Golem Korab, or Mount Korab (9,068 feet or 2,764 m), rises in this region on the Albania—North Macedonia border. Further south, the region contains Lake Ohrid and the Prespa Lakes (Great and Small). These large mountain lakes straddle Albania's borders with its neighbors. It shares Lake Ohrid with North Macedonia, and Lake Prespa is split three ways, among Albania, North Macedonia, and Greece.

WORLD HERITAGE SITES

Since 1975, the United Nations Educational, Scientific and Cultural Organization (UNESCO) has maintained a list of international landmarks or regions considered to be of "outstanding value" to the people of the world. Such sites embody the common natural and cultural heritage of humanity, and therefore deserve particular protection.

The organization works with the host country to establish plans for managing and conserving these sites. UNESCO also reports on sites which are in imminent or potential danger of destruction and can offer emergency funds to try to save the property.

The organization is continually assessing new sites for inclusion on the World Heritage list. In order to be selected, a site must be of "outstanding universal value" and meet at least one of ten criteria. These required elements include cultural value—that is, artistic, religious, or historical significance—or natural value, including exceptional beauty, unusual natural phenomena, or scientific importance.

The remains of an ancient theater are part of the ruins of the ancient city of Butrint.

As of January 2020, there were 1,121 sites listed: 869 cultural, 213 natural, and 39 mixed (cultural and natural) properties in 167 nations. Of those, 53 were listed as "in danger."

Albania is home to two cultural sites, one natural site, and one mixed. The cultural sites are Butrint, an archaeological site in southern Albania, and the Historic Centers of Berat and Gjirokaster in the central part of the country. The natural site, Ancient and Primeval Beech Forests of the Carpathians and Other Regions of Europe, is spread over 12 countries. The mixed site, Natural and Cultural Heritage of the Ohrid Region, covers the entire Lake Ohrid vicinity and is shared by Albania and North Macedonia. The Ohrid World Heritage site at first covered only the part of the lake located in North Macedonia, but the site was extended in 2019 to include the Albanian side as well.

The turquoise waters of the Ionian Sea add to the Mediterranean beauty of the Albanian coastal town of Sarande.

SOUTHERN MOUNTAIN REGION   Unlike the densely forested mountains of the north and central regions, the mountains of southern Albania are largely barren or sparsely covered with Mediterranean shrubs, oaks, and pines. Gorges, mountain streams, and valleys weave their way through these mountains, making this an area of great variety and beauty. The coastal mountains begin at the Bay of Vlore and run southward, rising dramatically to Mount Cika, 6,710 feet (2,045 m), then plunging to the Delvine District and the coastal town of Sarande. The coastal area of this region is known as the Albanian Riviera.

CLIMATE

Albania's climate is classified as mild and temperate, with cool, wet winters. Its average low temperature in January, its coldest month, is 41 degrees Fahrenheit (5 degrees Celsius). Its summers are hot and dry, with an average July temperature of 77°F (25°C).

WETLANDS, LAKES, AND RIVERS

Albania is a country rich in wetlands. Lagoons, lakes, rivers, and swamps, both saltwater and freshwater, are abundant. It has four major wetland areas that are of international importance under the Ramsar Convention. These are the Buna River and Lake Shkoder region, the Prespa Lakes, Lake Butrint, and Karavasta Lagoon, a part of Divjake-Karavasta National Park. These areas have rich biodiversity.

The Karavasta Lagoon, an important bird area, is home to a population of Dalmatian pelicans. The Velipoje wetland, part of the Buna River—Velipoje Protected Landscape in northwestern Albania, is also important for migratory birds, such as herons, ducks, and waders of many different species.

LAKES   Albania has 247 natural lakes and more than 800 artificial, or human-made, lakes. Lake Shkoder (also known as Lake Skadar or Lake Scutari), is the largest lake on the Balkan Peninsula. It covers 142 square miles (368 sq km) in the northwestern part of the country, with half of its waters in Albania and half in Montenegro.

A small part of Lake Shkoder is visible in the distance in this view of the surrounding countryside near the city of Shkoder.

The Ramsar Convention on Wetlands is an international treaty for the conservation and sustainable use of wetlands. The treaty dates to 1971 and is named for the Iranian city of Ramsar, where it was signed. The convention uses a broad definition of wetlands— it includes all lakes and rivers, underground aquifers, swamps and marshes, wet grasslands, peatlands, oases, estuaries, deltas and tidal flats, mangrove forests and other coastal areas, coral reefs, and all human-made sites such as fish ponds, rice paddies, reservoirs, and salt pans.

Wetlands are of vital importance, according to the Ramsar Convention, because they are among the world's most productive environments. They are ecosystems of "biological diversity that provide the water and productivity upon which countless species of plants and animals depend for survival."

As part of its mission, the convention identifies wetland sites around the world that are of international importance and works to protect them. Of the more than 2,300 Ramsar sites that have been designated, Albania has four, with a combined surface area of 242,610.5 acres (98,181 hectares). These are the Albanian Prespa Lakes, the Lake Butrint region, the Karavasta Lagoon ecosystem (shown above), and the Lake Shkoder/Buna River region.

Lake Fierza in the northeast, near the Kosovo border, is a reservoir that was formed by the construction of a dam and hydroelectric power plant along the Drin River.

The Lure Lakes are a group of 12 glacial lakes in the Lure Mountains at an altitude of about 5,250 feet (1,600 m). They are part of Lure National Park.

Lake Ohrid is the deepest lake in the Balkans. It overlaps the border between Albania and North Macedonia, with 42 square miles (110 sq km)

in Albania. The lake and its surrounding region in both countries is a UNESCO World Heritage site.

The Great Prespa Lake (sometimes called Lake Prespa) sits at the meeting point of Albania, North Macedonia, and Greece. The Albanian portion is a national park characterized by great biodiversity. To its southeast lies Small Prespa Lake, which is mostly in Greece but which extends a bit into Albania. It is home to the world's largest breeding colony of Dalmatian pelicans.

Lake Butrint is named for the ancient city of Butrint, another World Heritage site. The lake is a salt lagoon overlooking the Ionian Sea near the city of Sarande in the southern coastal region of Albania.

RIVERS   Albania has more than 150 rivers and streams. Most rivers originate in the mountainous eastern part of the country and flow to the Adriatic Sea. The longest river is the Drin (or Drini), 175 miles (280 km) of which flow through Albania. The river starts at the confluence of it two headwaters, the Black Drin and the White Drin, both of which arise outside of Albania.

Dalmatian pelicans fly over one of the Prespa Lakes.

Other important rivers are the Vjose (or Vjosa), the Shkumbin, the Mat, the Erzen, the Seman (or Semani), the Ishem (or Ishmi), and the Buna (or Bojana). Of these, only the Buna is navigable.

FLORA

Much of Albania's flora is evergreen, from Mediterranean scrub and flowering plants along the coastal lowlands to Alpine firs in the northern mountain region. More than 3,200 kinds of plants grow in Albania, and over a quarter of the land is forested.

The coastal strip is covered with maquis, a typical Mediterranean scrub bush. In the north, the coastal plain is cultivated farmland. The southern coastal plain is much hillier and has been terraced with citrus and olive groves. Deciduous forests, mostly beech and oak, cover higher elevations. Just below the tree line at about 6,560 feet (2,000 m) grow forests of birch, pine, and fir. Above them, the landscape consists of mountain pastures.

FAUNA

Albania's geographical location is responsible for its richly diverse animal population. It is located on the migration route of many birds. BirdLife International lists 302 types of birds found in Albania, including grouse, woodcocks, snipes, and pelicans. One bird, the slender-billed curlew, is listed as critically endangered, but it might already be extinct. The country also serves as a feeding ground for migrating birds traveling between northern Africa and Europe on the Adriatic Flyway.

Land animals include carnivorous brown bears, wolves, foxes, jackals, lynx, and wildcats among Albania's 58 species of mammals. Herbivores include wild goats, deer, and hares. Freshwater fish thrive in the lakes and rivers. The most common are sardine, mullet, red mullet, carp, and speckled trout.

This view from the Greek island of Corfu shows the Ionian Sea and the nearby Albanian coast.

TIRANA

Tirana is the capital city of Albania, founded as a settlement early in the 17th century by Ottoman Turks. Although not much more than a village as late as 1920, it was chosen as the capital primarily because of its central location. When the Italians exerted their influence over the city, they brought their sense of style with them, expanding the city center and building wide boulevards and substantial, elegant ministry buildings, hotels, and palaces. Construction continued during the communist era, and today, communist slogans can still be seen built into the brickwork of some of the buildings.

Tirana is a city of about 485,000 people and is the political and cultural center of the country. Young people from all over Albania have moved to this city, drawn to its increasingly lively nightlife.

Dajti, a mountain in the Skanderbeg range, towers over the capital city of Tirana.

EARTHQUAKE!

A 6.4-magnitude earthquake struck Albania on November 26, 2019. It was the strongest earthquake to hit Albania in 40 years. The earthquake killed 51 people, making it the country's deadliest earthquake in 99 years, and the world's deadliest in 2019. Around 3,000 were injured, and hundreds were left homeless. The epicenter was near the coastal city of Durres, where 25 people were killed and 900 buildings were damaged. In nearby Tirana, the earthquake damaged around 1,465 buildings. Search and rescue teams (shown below) arrived quickly from numerous European countries, as did 250 troops from Europe and the United States. The region experienced more than 1,000 aftershocks, which hindered some of those search efforts.

A 5.6-magnitude earthquake had struck the same general area just two months earlier. The region is seismically active. Albania sits on the convergent boundary, or fault line, between two of Earth's tectonic plates—the Eurasian Plate and the Adriatic Plate. The deep underground collisions can lead to earthquakes and other disruptions.

Albania's Independence Day celebrations, usually held on November 28, were canceled that year, and the country observed a national day of mourning instead.

Tirana International Airport Nene Tereza (Mother Teresa Airport), outside of Tirana, is Albania's only commercial international airport. Its flights are primarily to other destinations in Europe. Railroads provide cheap but slow connections to other cities.

DURRES

Durres, the second-largest city in Albania, lies on the Adriatic Sea. It is in a fertile region in which corn, grain, sugar beets, and tobacco are grown and livestock is raised. An important commercial and communications center serving central Albania, the city has a power plant, a dockyard, and factories producing bricks, cigarettes, leather products, and soap. Exports include grain, hides, minerals, and tobacco. The city is linked by rail with Tirana and Elbasan.

Durres is the seat of an Eastern Orthodox metropolitan, the primary church official in the province, and since the fifth century CE, of a Roman Catholic archbishop. Outside the city are remains of Byzantine and Venetian fortifications.

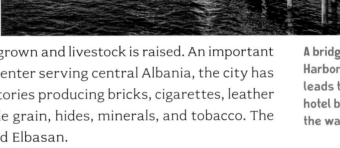

A bridge in Ventus Harbor, Durres, leads to a luxury hotel built out over the water.

SHKODER

Shkoder (or Shkodra) was founded around the fourth century BCE and is one of Albania's oldest cities. In the far north of the country, it sits on the eastern shore of Lake Shkoder, which spans the border between Albania and Montenegro. The Buna River flows from the lake to the Adriatic Sea. Initially, Shkoder was a tribal center and grew into a capital of the Illyrian kingdom. Over the next thousand years, it was an important military and trading hub, a Serbian center, and a Venetian possession.

During the 300 years that followed, it resisted and then fell to the Ottoman Turks, finally becoming the economic center of northern Albania, producing silk, tobacco, arms, and silver. During those years, Shkoderns built the stone houses that came to be thought of as typically Albanian—two-story houses with shops or stables on the ground floor and living quarters above. They also built an arched bridge, Mesi, that still stands.

By the 18th century, Shkoder was also the center of Turkish influence and administration. A lively bazaar was the center of city life. Throughout the 19th century, there were many uprisings against the Turks, but Ottoman rule held firm. At the same time, by mid-century, there were more than 3,500 shops in Shkoder, and it was an important center of trade for the entire Balkan Peninsula, with a trade administration, a trade court, and an international postage system.

Shkoder was active in the fight for Albanian independence and struggled mightily against attempts of countries like Montenegro, Serbia, and ultimately Yugoslavia to claim it. Shkoderns fought against the Italians in World War II and were in the forefront of the battle against the communists in 1990 and 1991, fighting against the police in demonstrations and riots.

Today, with a population of 135,600 people, Shkoder is back where it started, an important cultural and economic center of trade. It has flourishing electronics, food processing, and building materials industries. Other industries include wood and leather processing, textiles and clothing, and tobacco.

As a cultural center, Shkoder is home to a university, a large library, theater and dance groups, and many museums.

Two very different architectural styles exist in Shkoder. One is old, with narrow streets bordered by high stone walls with gates at each end. However, the main part of the city was rebuilt after World War II in the communist-era style of straight, wide streets with blocks of residential and public buildings. A large industrial park has grown up north of the city.

Shkoder has over 90 cultural monuments. Many are Turkish, such as the Turkish Bath and the Plumbi Mosque, but the most important is Rozafa Castle. Much of the castle's surviving structure was built by Venetians during the Middle Ages, but some remains on the site date to ancient times.

OTHER CITIES

Elbasan, Vlore, and Korce are other important Albanian cities. During the communist years, they were centers of manufacturing, but during the unrest following the communist collapse in 1992 and the economic collapse in 1997, many of the factories were damaged or destroyed, and few have reopened. Still, the cities have enormous historical, religious, and cultural meaning for the people and have been homes to families stretching back through the centuries.

The red and black flag of Albania flies over historic Rozafa Castle. Shkoder is seen in the distance.

INTERNET LINKS

http://livingbuna.org
Information on the Buna River—Velipoje Protected Landscape can be found on this website.

https://www.lonelyplanet.com/albania
This travel site looks at the top attractions in Albania.

https://www.ramsar.org/wetland/albania
This is the Ramsar page for Albania.

https://www.theguardian.com/cities/2018/oct/29/tirana-2030 -albania-capital-plan-erion-veliaj
This article looks at Tirana's plans for development and modernization.

https://whc.unesco.org/en/statesparties/al
This is the World Heritage listing page for Albania.

HISTORY

The giant stone head of Roman emperor Constantine the Great guards Berat Castle, overlooking the town of Berat in southern Albania.

2

THE HUMAN HISTORY OF ALBANIA begins in the Paleolithic period, roughly 100,000 to 10,000 BCE. Tools retrieved from along the Ionian Sea show that an ancient civilization existed at the foot of Mount Dajti near Tirana.

Around 5000 BCE, a settlement in the southern coastal area left the remains of huts, earthenware, and tools. The civilization associated with the Cakran settlement also left vases decorated with painted motifs of human beings. The most important ancient Albanian culture, though, was the Illyrians, a loosely formed group of Mediterranean tribes who were ancestors to the peoples of classical Rome and Greece.

From its beginnings, the written history of Albania is a story of hundreds of years of invasions and migrations. In the third century BCE, an Illyrian tribe, the Ardiaeans, established itself at Shkoder, a city in the northern mountains of today's Albania. The Illyrians were known not only as brave and skilled warriors but also as socially evolved and hospitable people. Men and women were of near equal status in the community, with women serving as heads of tribal federations. Illyrians believed in an afterlife. They buried weapons and personal items with the dead for use in the next world. The land was rich in iron, copper, gold, and silver, and Illyrians were skilled miners and metalsmiths. They were also accomplished shipbuilders and sailors. One of their designs became the prototype for the Roman liburna, an especially fast and light warship.

ALBANIA UNDER THE ROMANS

Rome recognized the Illyrian territories as valuable to their expansion plans to lands east of the Adriatic. In 229 BCE, they began their assault on Illyrian lands, and by 168 BCE, Illyria was part of the Roman Empire.

For the next six centuries, Rome ruled Illyrian lands. Roman culture and language had a great influence on Illyrian culture, especially in what is now southern Albania. Through the Romans, Christianity came into the culture, where it competed with Illyrian pagan beliefs and cults from the East. As the Roman Empire declined, people of Illyrian descent grew in influence and power, especially in the military.

Theodosius the Great was the last Roman emperor to rule over the entire Roman Empire. Theodosius established Christianity as the religion of the empire and did away with all remaining expressions of the old Roman religion. After his death, the eastern part of the Roman Empire broke away and became the Byzantine Empire. Albania fell into this empire.

During the first 70 years of Byzantine rule, the region battled raiders from the north, Visigoths, Huns, and Ostrogoths. Then came the Slavs. Though most of the Balkans buckled culturally as well as militarily in the face of the invaders, the Illyrians of modern-day Albania resisted assimilation, maintaining their language and many of their ways. Sometime between the sixth and eighth centuries CE, the name Illyria gave way to Albanoi, after an Illyrian tribe in what is today central Albania. The name spread from central Albania and was taken up by people throughout the land.

Despite being part of the Byzantine Empire, Albanian Christians remained, at first, under the jurisdiction of the pope in Rome. In 732 CE, however, the Byzantine emperor Leo III placed the Albanian church under the patriarch of Constantinople, the seat of Byzantine Christianity (in today's Istanbul, Turkey). When the Christian church split in 1054 over doctrinal disagreements, the Eastern Church broke away from Roman Catholicism for good, becoming the Eastern Orthodox Church. Southern Albania retained its tie to Constantinople, while northern Albania remained loyal to Rome. This schism in Albanian religion would be further challenged by the arrival of Islam in a few more centuries.

BYZANTINE RULE

The late Middle Ages marked the height of Albanian urban culture. International trade flourished between Albanian cities and European cities in Italy, Croatia, and Greece. The resulting prosperity stimulated growth in education, art, and literature. Significantly, though, Greek and Latin, not Albanian, were the languages used in cultural and government circles.

Likewise, the Byzantine system of government broke down tribal loyalties and strengths. The land was divided into themes, or military territories. Young men were conscripted for service by their military landlords and returned home to work the land as serfs. An aristocracy formed, especially in the south, rivaling the kinship loyalties of the Illyrian tribes.

Byzantine rule lasted nearly 1,000 years in Albania, but by the end of the 14th century—following raids and rule by Bulgarians, Norman crusaders, Italians, Venetians, and finally, Serbs—thousands of Albanians had emigrated, and the country was ripe for picking by the Turks. Whereas the Romans had traveled through Albania as a route to the East, Turkey saw it as a stepping-stone to the West.

By this time, the religion of Islam, born in Arabia in the 7th century, had spread far beyond the Arab world. Arab Muslim armies swiftly conquered territories in neighboring lands. By the early 1300s, most of the Byzantine Empire was supplanted by the Ottoman Empire, a Muslim-led empire named for the Turkish tribal leader Osman I.

A statue of the hero Skanderbeg stands in Kruje, a town that was once the capital of the Kingdom of Albania. The town is the location of the historic Kruje Castle, which houses the National Skanderbeg Museum.

SKANDERBEG AND THE RESISTANCE

The Ottomans soon looked to the Balkans, and the invasion began in 1388. Then came the resistance that has shaped Albanian pride and identity, a 25-year standoff led by Gjergj (George) Kastrioti, known to Albanians as Skanderbeg. Born in Albania in 1405, Kastrioti was conscripted into the Turkish army, where he gained notoriety as a military genius. In 1443, he deserted the Turks and came home as Skanderbeg to unify and lead the Albanian princes in driving out the invaders. For 25 years, from his boyhood home of Kruje, Skanderbeg and his army held off the Turks, providing the only real resistance the Ottoman Empire met in its sweep through the Balkans. It was a hopelessly unequal fight, and its 25-year duration won Skanderbeg and his Albanians the admiration of Europeans.

Skanderbeg's success was stunning. After his death in 1468, however, the unity he had inspired among the Albanians collapsed, and with it the organized resistance. By 1506, the Turks were in complete control of the country and would remain so for the next 400 years.

The Renaissance that would enlighten and shape the rest of Europe was just beginning when the Turks took control of Albania. This was the first stage of Albania's withdrawal from the rest of Europe, as it was cut off from the exchange of ideas that shaped Europe's humanistic future.

TURKISH RULE

Turkish rule was harsh. To escape persecution, one-fourth of the Albanian population fled to southern Italy, Sicily, and the Dalmatian coast. Yet the Turks were never able to fully crush the Albanian spirit. Especially in the northern highlands, they ruled in name only. Tribal authority and loyalty governed the highlanders, and they did not pay taxes, serve in the army, or turn in their arms. Their uprisings were frequent and fierce.

In response to Albanian resistance, and believing it to be religiously motivated, the Turks embarked on a program of enforced conversion to Islam. By the end of the 17th century, two-thirds of the Albanian people had become Muslims, many to avoid the enormous taxes levied on Christians. Christianity itself had resulted in religious fragmentation of the population between followers of Rome and Constantinople, and the forced conversions to Islam further politicized the notion of religion. Hundreds of years later, Albanian nationalists would proclaim, "The religion of Albania is Albanianism," in an effort to promote unity.

The Turks ruled Albania under a feudal system that awarded land to military lords who served them well. Over time, these lords assumed more autonomy. They became known as pashas, and for several generations two families established separate states in northern Albania and in southern Albania and Greece, ruling until the 19th century, when they were overthrown by Turkey once again.

The rule of the pashas now fell to private landowners, known as beys, in the south, and to tribal chieftains in the northern highlands. Peasants in the south worked as tenant farmers for the beys. Albanians in the north lived in patriarchal societies. Many Albanians left the country to advance themselves. Some, however, stayed within the Ottoman Empire and attained high positions in government and the military.

The Monument of Independence in Vlore depicts Ismail Qemali, the leader of the national movement and the first prime minister of Albania.

In the 19th century, the Turks were beginning to lose their grip on the Balkan countries. In 1878, Albanians living in several Balkan countries met in Kosovo and formed the Prizren League (or Albanian League). Their first goal, which would be unsuccessful, was to unite Albanians throughout the Balkans into an autonomous Albanian entity.

Their second goal was more successful, though it would take nearly 50 years to realize. It was to restore the Albanian language. The Prizren League became a powerful symbol to Albanians for their national aspirations, even though it was suppressed by the Turks for its politics. In 1908, the league met again to adopt a national language and alphabet, which replaced several variations. The national movement now represented the feelings of most Albanians, and when the Turks in 1908 reneged on promises for democratic reform, the Albanians took up arms. After three years of battle, from 1910 to 1912, Albania declared its independence on November 28, 1912.

THE GREAT POWERS

In December 1912, a group of ambassadors from Britain, Germany, Russia, Austria-Hungary, France, and Italy, known as the Great Powers, met in London, England, to deal with issues raised by Albanian independence. Though they recognized the independence of Albania, and thus its right to exist as a separate state, they ignored the ethnic realities of the region. Instead of uniting the Albanians of Albania, Greece, and Kosovo, they ceded Kosovo to neighboring Serbia and the southern lands to Greece. This left half of the Albanian people outside the borders of the new state. While excluding many Albanians, the Great Powers included 35,000 Greeks within Albanian's borders. To this day, both Kosovo and the Greek population of Albania are troublesome issues.

WORLD WAR I

The Great Powers also appointed a German prince to rule Albania, but he was woefully unprepared. Within six months of his appointment, World War I had broken out, and he gladly went home. As part of the war effort, the armies of Austria-Hungary, France, Italy, Greece, Montenegro, and Serbia invaded and occupied Albania, which by this time had assumed its present size. By the time the war ended, Albania was in chaos, without leaders or a real government. At the Paris Peace Conference after the war, Britain, France, and Italy proposed to partition Albania among its bordering countries. Only the veto of US president Woodrow Wilson kept the tiny country from being gobbled up. (Streets all over Albania are named after Woodrow Wilson in honor of his help.) In 1920, an Albanian national congress formed a new government. In December of that year, Albania—this time with the help of Britain—was admitted to the League of Nations and was recognized for the first time as a sovereign nation.

Now Albania's challenge was to reconcile two very different groups. One was composed of conservative landowners from the Ottoman past, led by a chieftain from the north-central part of the country, Ahmed Bey Zogu. The other group was led by Fan S. Noli, a bishop of the Orthodox Church who had been educated in the United States. His group was largely liberal and pro-democratic, consisting mainly of politicians, merchants, and intellectuals who were relying on the West and on Albanian communities there to help modernize their country and lead them into the 20th century. Neither leader could bridge the gap caused by competing factions and goals.

Still, the liberal forces gathered strength and unified their appeal. In 1924, there was a successful peasant revolt, and Zogu sought refuge in neighboring Yugoslavia. Noli became prime minister and set out to build a Western-style democracy in Albania, embarking on a program of land reform. However, he was slow in carrying out his program, his treasury was depleted, and his government was too liberal to gain international support. After just six months, he was overthrown in a revolt led by the returning Zogu.

KING ZOG

Zogu thus began a 14-year reign in Albania—first as president (1925—1928), then as King Zog I (1928—1939). The social base of Zog's power was a coalition of southern

King Zog, pictured here sometime between 1928 and 1930, was a self-proclaimed monarch with no ties to any existing royal family. He did, however, claim to be related, through his mother's side, to the national hero Skanderbeg.

beys, landowners, and northern *bajraktars*, or tribal leaders. With the support of his coalition, an efficient police force, and Italian financing, King Zog brought stability to Albania. Under his rule, the tribes of the highlands acknowledged the central government's authority. The rampant lawlessness that had characterized the country was curbed. The society of the cities began to show some similarity to the social life of Western countries, and he initiated universal education, at least in concept.

However, his rule was characterized by failure because he did not carry out a policy of land reform. The people of Albania were left as impoverished in independence as they had been as a Turkish colony. Moreover, though his country was formally a constitutional monarchy, it was actually just a dictatorship. As had happened so often before, thousands of Albanians migrated to other countries. Those who remained grew increasingly disillusioned as Zog continued to thwart democratic rule. Eventually, Zog's rule alienated most of the intellectual class and caused unrest among the working classes. His refusal to accommodate democracy and his failure to make the economy work led to the formation of communist groups in Albania.

The country was unstable both politically and socially. Zog signed several accords with Italy to bring financial relief to Albania, but they had only a short-term effect and did not expand the economy, especially since the world was by now in the midst of the Great Depression. On the very tenuous basis of these accords, in 1939, the fascist government of Italy invaded and occupied the country. King Zog fled once again, this time to Greece.

WORLD WAR II

In the meantime, World War II had broken out. Italy's occupation of Albania gave it a base for invading Greece, but the Greeks rebuffed the attack. The Italians withdrew back into Albania. The Germans were more successful in taking over Greece and Yugoslavia, bringing about a reunion of the Albanian regions of Greece and Kosovo with Albania. The Germans also replaced the Italians as the occupying force in Albania. On the verge of losing the war, Germany withdrew from Albania. In November 1944, Kosovo was returned to Yugoslavia, and Cameria, which was the Greek part of Albania, reverted to Greece.

Throughout World War II, the Albanian resistance was fiercely active against the Italian and the German occupiers. The resistance was largely composed of members of the communist groups that had formed in opposition to King Zog, and now these groups became one party, the Albanian Communist Party, under the leadership of Enver Hoxha. On November 29, 1944, the Communist Party seized control of the government. As secretary-general of his party, Enver Hoxha became prime minister. In 1946, the country renamed itself the People's Republic of Albania.

PEOPLE'S REPUBLIC

When World War II ended, the Albanian government feared that Yugoslavia, which had helped install the Albanian Communist Party, was moving to annex or otherwise assume power in Albania. Once again faced with loss of autonomy,

For nearly 50 years, the government and life in Albania was defined and controlled by Enver Hoxha. Born in 1908, Hoxha distinguished himself in World War II as a leader of the resistance against occupation and a founder of Albania's Communist Party. Nationalistic to the point of paranoia, he increasingly isolated his country, first from the Western countries, and in the end from former allies China and the Soviet Union. In his lifetime, Hoxha held the positions of first secretary of the Albanian Communist Party, premier of Albania, minister of foreign affairs, and commander in chief of the army, sometimes all at one time.

Hoxha's brand of communism was a fervent devotion to the Marxist-Stalinist ideal of centralized power in both government and economy. The population of postwar Albania was made up of subsistence farmers—80 percent of whom were illiterate—living without electricity or plumbing, and with a life expectancy of 40 years. Hoxha brought education and industry to the country by creating schools, relocating workers to factories, and collectivizing farms. Executions and imprisonment eliminated all opposition, whether actual, potential, or imaginary.

Ill health in the last 10 years of his life kept Hoxha from day-to-day rule, but his authority was so well established that his subordinates carried on his ideas in his name, and no other ruler took his place. He spent these later years writing theory and memoirs that articulated the position that increasingly isolated him and his country from the rest of the world, a belief in the absolute power of the state. When he died in 1985, many Albanians cried, for fear that they would be arrested if they did not. By then, the literacy rate was nearly 100 percent, and life expectancy had increased to over 70 years. At the same time, however, Albania was the poorest country in Europe.

the government established the form of control that would persist for the next 50 years, a Soviet-style political dictatorship. While Soviet leader Joseph Stalin lived, Albania and the Soviet Union were mutually supportive, but when Stalin died, the Albanian government lost faith in the Soviet Union's ability to safeguard Albania's independence. Though the Soviet Union remained staunchly communist, during the late 1950s it rejected some of the excesses of Stalinism. The other countries in Eastern Europe began to exhibit a diversity that was alarming to Albania's more conservative government, which was still fiercely devoted to Stalinist policies.

To solidify its power, the Hoxha government conducted purges of the moderates within the party. Thousands were executed or imprisoned. A campaign to minimize foreign influence further isolated Albania from the outside world. The government moved people living in the cities to the countryside to work on collective farms to discourage association between intellectuals and activists.

A POLICE STATE

Albania was now a police state. Strict obedience and conformity were expected and enforced. All dissent was repressed. Religion was illegal, and Albania proclaimed itself the world's first officially atheist nation. Travel was severely limited within—and forbidden outside—the country. It was illegal to own a car. Even naming babies was regulated. Parents consulted a list of acceptable names that changed each year. Sometimes the names were made up, like Marenglen, which is composed of the first three letters of Marx, Engels, and Lenin—three important figures in the development of communism. Wives of disgraced party members were forced to divorce their husbands. Complaining about food shortages was cause for family imprisonment.

A secret police force, called the Sigurimi, monitored all activity. Neighbors and family members became spies, with children trained to spy on parents. Punishable crimes included listening to banned radio programs or expressing disrespect for Enver Hoxha. If one person was found in violation of the law, the whole family, parents and grandparents as well, could be sent to a prison camp, where they would be tortured and sometimes allowed to starve to death.

Today, the National Historical Museum lists the toll of Hoxha's reign as 17,900 imprisoned, 5,157 killed, and 30,383 exiled. Many Albanians think these numbers woefully understate the reality. They believe that hundreds of thousands of people disappeared into the prison camp system, where they were killed or worked to death.

ISOLATION

As its relations with the Soviet Union faltered, Albania forged ties with China, both out of admiration for China's Cultural Revolution and in recognition that the two countries were so far apart that China couldn't possibly invade. Until about 1976, China provided some economic assistance to Albania, but that ended when Chinese leader Mao Zedong died. For the next 15 years, Albania had virtually no allies or partners. Its people were so isolated that some thought they were living in the most prosperous and advanced country in Europe.

During these years, the Albanian economy declined. A lack of trading partners meant that whatever Albania could not produce could not be had. Machinery and technology wore out and became outdated. As a result, industrial and agricultural productivity fell, though the demands made on workers kept production levels higher than they might otherwise have been. Although the early years of industrialization had led to advances over the prewar years in the supply of electricity and infrastructure, the systems deteriorated as the economy failed to support them.

After Hoxha's death in 1985, the country was run by Ramiz Alia with little change in policy. Alia continued the pattern of isolation from both East and West. Domestically, he preserved inherited policies of religious persecution and political oppression.

Ramiz Alia, shown here on a visit to Paris in September 1991, served as Albania's head of state for 10 years.

WINDS OF CHANGE

In the late 1980s, change was in the wind throughout Eastern Europe and the Soviet Union. The flow of information had become somewhat harder to control as radio stations from neighboring countries broadcast news of change and development in the region. The median age of Albanians was just 25, and the young were cautiously looking for improvement. Perhaps most significantly, the limitations of a centrally controlled, underdeveloped, agrarian economy were becoming unavoidably clear—with the youthful population growing, the economy simply could not absorb them. Shortages of energy and imported materials prevented the industrial sector from expanding, though demand for industrial products remained high.

The government began to promote some changes. It instituted policies of worker incentives, rewarding productivity. It allowed limited criticism of government policies, though it was disinclined to make any changes based on such criticism, and workers were similarly disinclined to criticize. Workers who had seen nothing good come from overachieving or from critical thinking in the past met these tiny steps toward change with skepticism and fear. They did not believe that change could come from within the system.

By 1989, communism had all but collapsed throughout Eastern Europe, and the Albanian people became more difficult to control. Intellectuals, the working class, and the young began to agitate against the communist government. Alia lifted restrictions. He allowed people to travel abroad, permitted the free practice of religion, and adopted an open-market policy for the economy.

Finally, in December 1990, he allowed the creation of independent political parties. This was the end of the Communist Party monopoly on power. In 1992, Albanians elected a non-communist government, and Alia resigned as president. His replacement was Sali Berisha, head of the Democratic Party. Albania's international isolation was officially ended.

Sali Berisha was president of Albania from 1992 to 1997, and prime minister from 2005 to 2013.

PYRAMID SCHEMES

Albania's efforts to establish a free-market economy proceeded at an unsteady pace, but its progress brought international financial aid. In the following years, governments would rise and fall amid scandal and corruption.

In 1997, Albania suffered a breakdown of nearly all social order when its economy collapsed. During the previous years, the corrupt government had urged the citizens to invest their savings in what turned out to be a series of pyramid schemes. This sort of business operation is a form of investment (illegal in the United States and elsewhere) in which each participant pays to join and then recruits two further paying participants. Early investors, or those at the top of the pyramid, receive the money contributed by later ones, or those below them. What inevitably happens, though, is that the later investors can never find enough new ones, and the people at the bottom of the pyramid—that is, the majority of investors—lose their money. With that, the entire scheme collapses.

Nearly half of the citizens invested their life savings, a total of about $2 billion. When, inevitably, the schemes collapsed, the entire government and the citizenry were left bankrupt. Thousands of people rioted for months, destroying infrastructure the country could ill afford to lose or replace. Mobs raided military arms stores and weapons depots and stole thousands of weapons—Kalashnikov rifles, mines, and bombs. At least 1,500 people were killed. United Nations (UN) peacekeeping troops were brought in to subdue the civil disorder.

Complicating matters during a tough economic time, war broke out in neighboring Kosovo, then part of Serbia. Nearly half a million ethnic Albanians poured into Albania in 1999, seeking safety. Many were taken in by Albanian

Albanian protesters take to the streets on February 27, 1997, in Vlore.

families, while others stayed in camps. NATO sent 8,000 troops to Albania to help manage the crisis. Most refugees returned to Kosovo after the war.

REACHING OUT TO EUROPE

Coming out of the oppression and isolation of the Enver Hoxha era, Albania wanted to form closer relations with Europe. In particular, it sought to join NATO, and later, the European Union (EU). It began the NATO accession process in the early 1990s and finally joined the alliance in 2009. That same year, Albania applied for membership in the EU.

In 2010, the European Union rejected Albania's request for EU candidate status, but by 2014, it accepted Albania as a candidate. As such, the country was qualified to receive $1.3 billion in developmental aid and was expected

On October 18, 2019, Edi Rama, Albania's prime minister, vows to keep working on reforms after the EU Council failed to approve accession talks with Albania and North Macedonia.

to meet certain preconditions. One of those mandated that Albania make reforms to its justice system. Also, it was to institute a new electoral law, bring corrupt judges to trial, and demonstrate respect for the human rights of its Greek minority.

In 2019, the European Commission, the executive branch of the EU, said sufficient progress had been made and recommended that Albania open EU accession negotiations. This signaled a step forward in the process.

However, Albania's EU accession is bundled with that of its neighbor North Macedonia. In October 2019, both of those countries were unpleasantly surprised when the EU effectively said "no." All member states must unanimously agree in order for a country's accession process to begin. In this case, Denmark, the Netherlands, and France opposed Albania's application, and France alone blocked North Macedonia as well. Objections, led by France's president, Emmanuel Macron, were based on disagreements about the accession process itself. Macron said the EU body needed to address those issues before accepting any more members. But there was also widespread concern among EU members about corruption and illegal migration in the western Balkans.

INTERNET LINKS

https://www.bbc.com/news/world-europe-17681099
BBC News has a timeline of key events in Albania's history, beginning in 1939.

https://www.britannica.com/place/Albania
The online *Encyclopedia Britannica* provides a thorough overview of Albania's history.

https://www.nytimes.com/1985/04/12/world/enver-hoxha -mastermind-of-albania-s-isolation.html
The *New York Times* obituary of Enver Hoxha provides a good review of his life and influence.

GOVERNMENT

The Albanian flag on Gjirokaster Fortress waves over the castle's clock tower.

3

ALBANIANS CALL THEIR COUNTRY Shqiperia. The name derives from their language, called Shqip (SHKEEP). Albania is the English-language name, which comes from the ancient Illyrian tribe of the Albanoi (or Albani).

The Republic of Albania is an emerging democracy with a parliamentary system of government. As such, it operates under a constitution ratified in 1998, with a government chosen in free elections. Making the transition from a communist hermit state to a modern, democratic, fully engaged European country has not been easy, but the country has made great progress.

THE PROBLEM OF FREEDOM

Centuries of Ottoman rule, followed by the authoritarian government of a self-proclaimed king, and then by 50 years of isolation under one of the most repressive communist governments in the world, left Albanians inexperienced in self-government. Even free thought was an unknown concept.

It might seem that offered the chance to decide their own destiny in all matters, people who had lived under tyrannical repression would gladly seize the opportunity. However, like people in other parts of the world living under tyranny, Albanians had developed priorities that superseded a desire for freedom. Foremost among these was a desire for safety. Freedom was viewed with fear and suspicion. It was seen as something

A double-headed eagle with its wings spread, the symbol of Albania, is featured against a red background on the nation's flag. The motif dates to the early Middle Ages and probably relates to an origin myth in which a young boy saves a baby eagle from being devoured by a snake. In return, the mother eagle rewards the boy with strength and courage. This legend establishes Albanians as "the children of eagles" and the country itself as the "Land of Eagles."

The Albanian flag, adopted in 1992, is a black, two-headed eagle on a red background. Its significance goes back to Skanderbeg. After abandoning the Turkish army, he returned to his father's home in Kruje. Above the castle, he flew a red flag with the double eagle, his family seal, as a symbol of his return. With the castle and the flag behind him, he proclaimed: "I have not brought you liberty. I found it among you." The Albanian nobles united behind him, and for the next 25 years, they held off the invading Turks. In modern times, the flag has variously borne a helmet, a hammer and sickle, and finally a star. After the fall of communism, the flag was returned to its original design.

that would lead to chaos and anarchy. Many Albanians were willing to trade a degree of freedom for greater safety.

To some extent, they were right. The difficulty of establishing a market economy or attracting foreign investment led to widespread unemployment. Government corruption and organized crime are serious problems not easily solved. In general, Albanians express dissatisfaction and mistrust in their government.

Though elections are free, the fiercely partisan nature of Albanian politics often results in boycotts of government institutions by one party or another. Opposition to government programs and officials can bring harassment at least, and often more severe reprisals. Government employees have been known to lose their jobs or be inconveniently transferred for expressing negative opinions or even failing to demonstrate sufficient enthusiasm.

THE CONSTITUTION

In 1994, Albanians were offered a new constitution to be ratified by referendum. The broadcast media, as clearly state-controlled as they had been under communism, relentlessly promoted its passage. The proposed constitution would have guaranteed Albanians most of the rights and freedoms other European countries had lived with since World War II or earlier. Though the constitution, to all who looked at it, seemed to be what they wanted, the vote represented a chance to show disapproval of the government. The people rejected the constitution.

The constitution finally passed in 1998, though the opposition boycotted the elections, and there were charges of widespread fraud and corrupt voting practices.

The constitution provides for free legislative elections every four years. All people ages 18 and over can vote. The constitution provides for essential human rights and freedoms—equality before the law and the freedoms of speech, the press, religion, and assembly. It also establishes the right to private property, the right to education and health care provided by the state, the right to form labor unions, and the right to strike.

How well the government enforces these rights is another question. Freedom House, an organization that tracks international trends in democracy, annually assesses each country's performance on political rights and civil liberties. In 2019, it found Albania to be "partly free," with an aggregate score of 68 out of 100, in which 100 equals "most free." (For perspective, the United States scored 86 that year; Finland, Norway, and Sweden were all awarded a perfect 100, while Syria rated a dismal 0.)

According to the report, Albanians generally enjoy freedom of religion and freedom of assembly. Freedom of speech and the press is somewhat compromised by the strong influence of business and political interests on the media, thereby preventing a free and independent media. In addition, the report points to corruption, particularly in the judiciary, and a lack of transparency in government and elections.

GOVERNMENT STRUCTURE

Tirana's Presidential Palace, or Palace of the Brigades, was designed by Italian architects in 1936 and completed in 1941. The architectural style, rationalism, is characterized by mathmatically based design: symmetry, simplicity, and a lack of ornamentation.

The president is the chief of state and is indirectly elected by the parliament for a five-year term. On the advice of the majority party in the parliament, the president appoints the prime minister, who is the head of the government. The prime minister selects a council of ministers, who are nominated by the president and then approved by the parliament.

The parliament is the unicameral, or one-house, legislature called the Assembly (Kuvendi). It's made up of 140 members who are divided among 12 districts. Within each district, each party puts forward a list of candidates, and seats in the assembly are divided among the parties based on their share of the vote. This is called a proportional-representation system. Representatives in the Assembly serve four-year terms.

The judicial system consists of two high courts, the Supreme Court and the Constitutional Court. The Supreme Court is the highest court of appeal; it consists of 19 judges, including the chief justice. These judges are appointed by the High Judicial Council, with the consent of the president, to serve a single nine-year term. They are not eligible for a second term. The Constitutional Court is the final authority for the interpretation of the constitution and the compliance of laws in accordance with the constitution. It has nine judges, who are appointed by the president, the Assembly, and the Supreme Court on a rotating basis. Like the Supreme Court judges, they serve nine-year terms that cannot be repeated.

In addition to the high courts, Albania's judiciary includes lower levels of subordinate courts, including courts of appeal and, at the primary level, district courts. There are also the Special Courts for Corruption and Organized Crime, which were established in 2019.

The Albanian Assembly Building in Tirana reflects the social realism style of architecture. It is characterized by the glorification of communist values and often incorporates massive decor elements such as tall, Greek-style columns. In 2011, Albania decided to construct a new building for the Assembly, which will "reflect democratic values" and have a highly modern design.

CORRUPTION

Albania is one of Europe's most corrupt countries, according to Transparency International (TI). The global anti-corruption organization, founded in 1993, defines corruption as "the abuse of entrusted power for private gain." They explain that corruption "can be classified as grand, petty and political, depending on the amounts of money lost and the sector where it occurs."

Corruption takes many forms, but one of the most common is bribery. TI defines bribery as "the offering, promising, giving, accepting or soliciting of an advantage as an inducement for an action which is illegal, unethical or a breach of trust. Inducements can take the form of gifts, loans, fees, rewards or other advantages (taxes, services, donations, favors etc.)."

As part of its mission, TI publishes the annual Corruption Perceptions Index (CPI), which assesses public sector corruption in countries around the world, rating each country with a score between 1 and 100—the lower the score, the greater the corruption. In 2019, Albania received a score of 35, tying it with Brazil, Mongolia, Côte d'Ivoire, North Macedonia, Algeria, and Egypt. Together, these countries were ranked 106th out of 180 countries evaluated by TI. (For context, New Zealand and Denmark tied for the number 1 spot as the world's least corrupt countries, each with a high score of 87, while Somalia took last place, with a score of 9.) Albania's corruption score was 5 points lower than it had been in 2016, indicating that the country's attempts to clean up were going backwards. Their 2019 scores gave Albania and neighboring North Macedonia the unhappy status of being some of Europe's most corrupt countries; only Moldova, Ukraine, and Russia were rated as more corrupt.

JUDICIAL SYSTEM REFORM

Albania has been actively trying to reduce corruption so that it can qualify for admission to the EU. Its judicial system is often identified as one of the most corrupt parts of the government. In 2016, the country launched the Judicial System Reform, an ambitious process to radically overhaul its courts.

As part of the process, all judges and prosecutors were required to be vetted, or investigated, on three things: the integrity of the assets accumulated

A woman shouts in favor of judicial reforms during a rally in front of the Albanian Assembly Building in Tirana on July 21, 2016.

during their career—in other words, whether their lifestyle matches their income—possible ties to organized crime, and professional misconduct.

As a result, so many judges were dismissed, or resigned rather than face the probe, that the court system was left without enough judges to operate. The Constitutional Court, for example, was left with only one out of nine judges, making it defunct, at least temporarily. In other courts, the backlog of cases grew by the thousands as the work of justice essentially ground to a halt.

The findings indicated that many judges could not justify their assets (money and property). Around 80 percent of the appeals court judges reportedly could not account for their assets during the period between 2004 and 2014. In fact, 25 judges of the appeals court in Tirana had assets worth more than $5.5 million, way above their monthly income. Such a disparity between income and assets strongly suggests corruption.

As of 2020, there were still hundreds of judges in Albania yet to be evaluated.

INTERNET LINKS

https://www.constituteproject.org/constitution/Albania_2016.pdf?lang=en
The constitution of Albania is available and downloadable on this page.

https://freedomhouse.org/report/freedom-world/2019/albania
Freedom House reports on the state of freedom in Albania.

https://www.ganintegrity.com/portal/country-profiles/albania
This site details the sorts of corruption plaguing Albania.

https://www.state.gov/u-s-relations-with-albania
The US State Department provides information about relations between the United States and Albania.

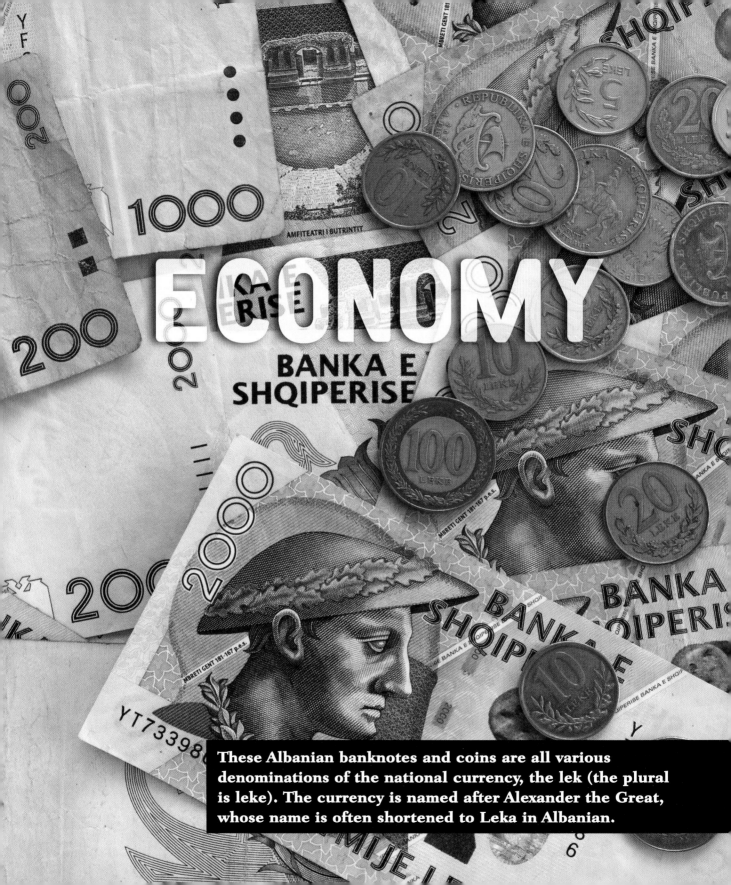

ECONOMY

These Albanian banknotes and coins are all various denominations of the national currency, the lek (the plural is leke). The currency is named after Alexander the Great, whose name is often shortened to Leka in Albanian.

4

ALBANIA IS STILL MAKING THE transition to a modern market economy. It has come a long way since emerging from half a century of communist isolation. When the Communist Party came to power in 1944, the country had no paved roads, virtually no electricity outside the cities, no industry, and a primitive, subsistence level of farming. Few people could read, and there was no public education.

Over the next 50 years, the government—largely in isolation, but with some economic help from the Soviet Union and China—developed cities, built factories, extended the availability of electric power, and organized agriculture into large, government-owned collective farms. School became mandatory for children for the first time in the country's history. Planning and organizing was centrally controlled, with goals and assignments set by the party.

COMMUNIST LEGACY

Central planning and government ownership were the key elements in Albania's communist economy. The good thing about the concept was that everybody shared equally in the wealth (at least in theory). The bad thing about the arrangement was that it did not produce much wealth.

Many high-level sources say that unofficially, Albania's top economic sector is narcotics. Organized crime, hand-in-hand with police and government corruption, has a powerful grip on Albania, making it what some call "Europe's first narco-state," or "the Colombia of Europe." Albanian drug-smuggling gangs and the Albanian "mafia" have spread through Europe, where they are known for their ruthlessness and violence.

Enver Hoxha's iron rule kept people from rebelling, and the system held firm, even though the country did not prosper. Individual effort and initiative were not rewarded, as everyone received the same small amount, regardless of their input. Albanians learned that there was nothing to gain from exerting themselves or from thinking creatively to solve problems. This attitude, a communist legacy, would be hard to adjust when the economic system changed.

When the communist government fell in 1990, it left a population totally without resources or experience in free-market economics. With the infrastructure falling apart and a lack of money or management skills, the people were left in an economic vacuum of sorts. Gross domestic product (GDP) fell 50 percent from what it had been in 1989. For many, there seemed to be only two options—emigrate or turn to crime. Many did emigrate, and many still do today. Since 1991, more than 1.4 million Albanians, nearly half the current population, have emigrated. Most went to neighboring Italy and Greece; however, when economic hard times hit both Italy and Greece in 2008, around 133,500 Albanian migrants returned home.

Organized crime found an easy foothold in a country with a fragile democracy, weak government, high unemployment and poverty, and a corrupt or cowed police force. As late as 2002, some police officers stopping cars to check for contraband wore hoods to protect themselves and their families from retaliation by organized crime members. Others hooded themselves to hide their identities so they could act without accountability. Police corruption remains a problem to this day.

In the early 1990s, the government embarked on an enthusiastic program to convert the economic system from centrally organized totalitarian control to a free-market system. To that end, they privatized most businesses, industries, and agriculture; encouraged outside investment; and liberalized prices and currency exchange. They also began to establish laws and banking practices that would conform to international expectations.

ECONOMIC COLLAPSE

In the 1990s, the government set up a series of pyramid schemes supposedly aimed at stimulating the economy. They encouraged the populace, fearful of

Gross domestic product (GDP) is a measure of a country's total production. The number reflects the total value of goods and services produced over one year. Economists use it to determine whether a country's economy is growing or contracting. Growth is good, while a falling GDP means trouble. Dividing the GDP by the number of people in the country determines the GDP per capita (per person). This number provides an indication of a country's average standard of living—the higher the better.

In 2017, the GDP per capita in Albania was approximately $12,500. That figure is considered low, and it ranked Albania 125th out of 228 countries listed by the CIA World Factbook. *For comparison, the United States that year was number 19, with a GDP per capita of $59,500. Only a few European countries ranked lower than Albania. They were Kosovo, at 137th, with a GDP per capita of $10,900; Ukraine, at 146th, with a GDP per capita of $8,800; and Moldova, at 162nd, with a GDP per capita of $6,700.*

disobeying authority and desperate for money, to invest their savings. They promised enormous returns on the investments. The early investors, mostly government functionaries and others who planned the programs, took their profits from the income generated by later investors. Ultimately and inevitably, the schemes collapsed, and the economy collapsed with them. Early investors fled with their profits or secreted them in foreign accounts, but most of the people of Albania lost everything.

The ensuing chaos left Albania resembling a country that had just lost a war. People rioted and destroyed buildings and infrastructure. The rule of law ceased to exist. Foreign aid workers who had supplied many social services were recalled home, and foreign investors lost any interest in Albania as a developing market or producer.

RECOVERY

Since then, the economy has slowly recovered. Since 2014, Albania's economy has steadily improved, and economic growth reached 4.1 percent in 2018. The economy continues to be hampered by poor infrastructure, complex tax codes and licensing requirements, a weak judicial system, endemic corruption, and poor enforcement of contracts and property issues. Also, although the data does not show up in official accounting systems, a great deal of Albania's economy is controlled by organized criminal activity in drug and human trafficking. This does not inspire international confidence in the country's ability to produce goods, make money, and protect investments.

In 2015, Albania launched an ambitious program to increase tax compliance and bring more businesses into the formal economy. In 2016, it passed constitutional amendments reforming the judicial system in order to strengthen the rule of law and reduce deeply entrenched corruption. As this process has gone forward, however, it has nearly paralyzed the judiciary, as hundreds of judges have either been dismissed or have resigned to avoid scrutiny.

The government also recognized the seriousness of its transportation problems. In the 2010s, it focused on improving the road infrastructure, urban transport, and air travel, and the results are a vast improvement. In 2018, the country acquired a new national airline carrier, Air Albania. As of 2020, it only operated flights from Tirana to Istanbul, Turkey, and to various cities in Italy.

The strongest driving force in reforming Albania's economy has been its desire to join the European Union.

NATURAL RESOURCES

Albania is rich in mineral resources. Gold has been mined in Albania since medieval times. A 2015 analysis determined the country's gold reserves to be about 14 million tons (12.7 metric tons). More important resources are oil, lignite, copper, chromium, limestone, salt, bauxite, and natural gas.

In 2019, Albania produced about 22,915 barrels of oil per day, making it the biggest producer in the western Balkans. (In the worldwide oil industry, an oil barrel is defined as 42 US gallons, which is about 159 liters.) It is also the largest exporter of crude oil in the region.

Mining, agricultural processing, and the manufacture of textiles, clothing, lumber, and cement are among the major industries. Chemical, iron, and steel plants were developed under communism, and some of them are still operating.

Some 1.15 million Albanians live and work outside the country—about 90 percent in Europe, and about 8 percent in the United States. This is a significant number of people, almost on par with the labor force within the country. In a country with an average unemployment rate of around 14 percent and a poverty rate of about 30 percent (according to the World Bank), it's not surprising that such a large number of people seek work abroad.

Many of those emigrant workers send a part of their earnings back home to family members. These transfers of money are called remittances, and they contribute a great deal to Albania's economy. In 2017 and 2018, Albanians abroad sent home about $1.27 billion per year, accounting for around 12 percent of the country's GDP. These funds helped 26 percent of Albanian families. Remittances, then, are a crucial sector of the economy.

ENERGY

Albania has more than a dozen hydroelectric plants that produce 95 percent of its electricity, but its hydropower relies completely on rainwater to keep rivers flowing at high volume, which leaves it vulnerable to weather extremes and climate change. In 2017, for example, a lack of rain caused output in the hydroelectric plants to fall by 37 percent.

Although Albania has committed to renewable energy sources, it has not fully explored solar and wind power. Only in 2017 did it begin to offer renewable energy incentives for the development of solar and wind energy.

After hydropower, the remaining 5 percent of Albania's electricity is generated by fossil fuels. However, that may soon change, as the country has plans to construct new gas power plants.

The Trans-Adriatic Pipeline (TAP), which began construction in 2016, is expected to increase demand for gas-fired energy in Albania. The TAP will follow a route from Greece to Albania and then across the Adriatic Sea to Italy. The TAP has been hailed (by the consortium of companies building it) as a great benefit to Albania. During the construction phase, the project created job opportunities for around 3,000 Albanians, and money was invested toward improving roads. After its expected completion in 2020, the pipeline will deliver gas to Albania and could possibly transform the country into a regional natural gas hub. The project also has its critics, mostly based on environmental concerns, but they have been more vocal in Italy and Greece than in Albania.

AGRICULTURE

Only about one-quarter of the mountainous country is farmland, but 41 percent of Albania's workforce is employed in agriculture. The sector contributes a significant 21.7 percent to the GDP. The main crops are grains, olives, fruits and vegetables, and sugar beets. The production of tobacco, which was widely grown during the country's communist years, has declined.

Grapes for winemaking are an important crop. Viticulture dates back approximately 6,000 years in Albania, and today the country is the 42nd-largest producer of wine in the world. Livestock is also raised to supply both meat and dairy products.

Agricultural fields cover the landscape of the Lake Shkoder region.

When farms were privatized in the early 1990s, the land was parceled out into small family farm units. What existing mechanized equipment the farms had was outdated and worn-out. The small landowners could not afford to replace or maintain this machinery, so they resorted to old-fashioned methods, such as using livestock to pull plows. Also, coming from a history of large-scale cooperatives, in which work was highly compartmentalized, the new family farmers lacked skills and knowledge. They were not trained in the modern farming technologies needed to run their businesses efficiently. Profitability was also affected by the difficulty of getting produce to market over Albania's poor road system.

Today, more than 90 percent of the 380,000 farms in Albania are below 5 acres (2 hectares) in size. Moving the country from subsistence farming to a modern agricultural industry requires a great deal of international aid. The European Union has become involved, as part of Albania's pre-accession process, to help the country raise its agricultural standards. Financial aid provides modern equipment and supports farmer education, the introduction of cooperatives, and the construction of collection and distribution centers.

TOURISM

The natural beauty of Albania's mountains and its long, sandy beaches offer the promise for the development of all kinds of tourism, and particularly for the development of the kind of elite resorts that exist elsewhere in Europe.

There are two main areas with potential for tourism development. Coastal zones, primarily the Adriatic coast from Velipoje to Vlore and the Ionian coast from Llogara to the Greek border, would be ideal for resorts and conference facilities. Interior zones, primarily lake and mountain areas, are suitable for more adventurous tourists who like to experience the country they are visiting.

Developing tourism is one of the Albanian government's main economic priorities, in the hope that it will account for a strong portion of the country's income in the near future. To that end, it has committed to rehabilitating and then maintaining the country's road network, developing and rehabilitating its ports in Durres and Vlore, building new ports, and opening airports that meet acceptable civil air standards to serve more cities than Tirana.

As Albania struggles to raise the level of its agricultural output, it's perhaps ironic that the government is trying to eliminate the country's most profitable crop. Albania was a major producer of marijuana, or cannabis, before a government crackdown in 2014. In fact, it was Europe's largest producer of outdoor-grown cannabis.

Cannabis is a plant indigenous to Central Asia, but it is now grown in almost every country on Earth. The plant has many uses. For example, one variety of cannabis can be made into hemp fiber, which is used in paper, textiles, biodegradable plastics, and other products. However, by far the best-known use of cannabis is in the making of recreational drugs. The plant contains several chemical substances—primarily THC—that have psychoactive properties, meaning that they affect brain function in people who consume them.

Special police destroy a field of cannabis plants in the village of Ducaj, a remote mountainous area of northern Albania. Villagers in the poor northern areas use plots of land in isolated regions to plant cannabis, in an effort to keep it hidden from police. Often, a bribe is necessary to keep the authorities from eradicating the illegal product.

For farmers in a poor country, the plant called "green gold" brought in tremendous profits. The problem is that growing cannabis is illegal in Albania, as it is in most countries. Although laws are changing rapidly, no European country (as of spring 2020) has legalized recreational use of marijuana.

In its bid for membership in the European Union, Albania pushed hard to eliminate this black-market sector of its economy. In 2014, an enormous police operation targeted the town of Lazarat, which is well known as the center of Albania's illegal drug industry. Using military-style force, the police seized many tons of cannabis, destroyed thousands of plants, and made more than 400 arrests. That year, they put a 30 percent dent in the illegal cannabis trade. However, without that level of law enforcement on a constant basis, it may have been for nothing. Reportedly, the business bounced back immediately.

The initiative has been working. In 2018, tourism and its related industries accounted for a very significant 26.2 percent of Albania's GDP. That same year, almost 6 million international tourists visited the country, an increase of 16 percent over the previous year. The number of tourists has been steadily increasing, as has the average length of their stays.

INTERNET LINKS

https://bankwatch.org/beyond-coal/energy-sector-in-albania
This site provides a quick overview of Albania's energy sector.

http://www.fao.org/family-farming/countries/alb/en
The UN Food and Agriculture Organization looks at the strengths and weakness of family farming in Albania.

**https://www.independent.co.uk/news/world/europe/albania-drug
-cannabis-trafficking-hub-europe-adriatic-sea-a8747036.html**
This in-depth report about the narcotics trade in Albania includes a video.

https://www.intellinews.com/outlook-2020-albania-173983
This business news site looks at Albania's economic situation in 2020.

**https://theculturetrip.com/europe/albania/articles/the-pyramid
-crisis-in-albania**
The circumstances that enabled Albania's pyramid scheme disaster are explored in this article.

**https://www.vice.com/en_us/article/zmpq89/the-inside-story-of
-europes-first-narco-state**
This site offers another look at Albania's narcotics connections.

ENVIRONMENT

The golden eagle is the symbol of Albania.

GIVEN ITS SMALL SIZE, ALBANIA'S wealth of ecosystems and habitats is impressive. Around 30 percent of Europe's plant species and 42 percent of Europe's mammals are found there. Albania is also an important bird area, with its variety of wetlands, lagoons, and large lakes that provide critical winter habitats for migratory birds.

However, today, Albania has one of Europe's highest rates of biodiversity loss, as deforestation, soil erosion, uncontrolled land use, and pollution take their toll. Unsustainable levels of hunting, fishing, and grazing are also threatening diversity.

As Albania seeks accession to the European Union, it is required to institute sustainable policies and achieve environmental goals across a variety of sectors. The country's main challenges include water and air pollution, land degradation and soil erosion, the loss of species, and unacceptable practices in waste management. Most of these problems are caused by human behavior; specifically, the European Environment Agency points to illegal logging, illegal fishing and wild animal hunting, and the inefficient management of recreation activities.

POLLUTION

Albania is rich in natural resources highly valued by other countries in Europe: expansive forests, fertile soil, and large freshwater supplies.

5

However, these resources were seriously degraded by unregulated industrial activities during Albania's communist years. Between 1944 and 1991, emission controls and wastewater treatment were not incorporated into most factory designs. In the agricultural collectives, where half of Albania's labor force worked, resources were invested in irrigating and fertilizing farmland, but environmental protection and soil conservation were not on the agenda.

In the years since the fall of communism, the demands on the poverty-stricken new democracy left few resources to allocate to the regeneration of the environment. In one regard, the environment actually benefited from the poor economy, as nearly half of the plants and factories closed and their contribution to the pollution of the air, water, and soil ceased.

At the same time, the influx of hundreds of thousands of refugees from Kosovo and other Balkan areas placed increased demands on a country where wastewater was released untreated into the sources from which it came. This

A water reservoir in Tepelene, in the south of Albania, is covered in orange algae.

situation has improved somewhat as the economy has improved and the wars in neighboring countries have come to an end. The long-term impact of the refugee situation was minimal.

CLEANUP EFFORTS

In 2003, the United Nations Environment Programme (UNEP) recognized five priority environmental hot spots for cleanup in Albania. Of those, a former chemical plant in the coastal city of Durres was identified as the most serious risk to human health, groundwater, and marine habitats. Hundreds of tons of chemicals and pesticides from an abandoned lindane factory had been left behind, contaminating the surrounding environment. The plant had produced pesticides for agriculture and chemicals for leather treatment. With international help from the Netherlands, Japan, and the World Bank, the site was demolished, and the chemicals and contaminated debris were shipped to a special disposal site in Germany. The project was completed in 2011 with the planting of trees and the construction of a playground on the site.

The other four sites identified as urgent matters were a fertilizer plant in Vlore, an oil refinery in Ballsh, the oil fields in Patos, and a solid waste dumpsite in Sharra. In all of these cases, the government worked with international environmental groups to improve conditions and clean up years of damage.

CHALLENGES

There is more to be done, though. The UN Economic Commission for Europe (UNECE) performed a second review in 2011 and a third one in 2018, to track Albania's progress in environmental matters. While the third review found improvement in many areas, it reported a broad lack of environmental awareness at national and local levels. The Albanian government has no overarching national policy, and few municipalities have adopted local environmental action plans. In fact, there is no overall budget for environmental protection.

PROTECTED AREAS

Albania has a system of parks and reserves, with 15 national parks, of which one is a marine park. The national parks feature a broad diversity of landforms, vegetation, and animal life. In addition, there are 2 nature reserves, 22 managed nature reserves, 5 protected landscapes, and 770 other protected areas of various categories.

Established in 2010, the Karaburun-Sazan Marine Park covers 49 square miles (126 sq km) of coastal lands in the Vlore region in the south. The park consists of a biologically rich terrain of mountains, canyons, bays, beaches, and underwater caves. Offshore, it features ruins of sunken ancient Greek, Roman, and World War II ships. The park also includes Albania's largest island,

Sazan Island, which is only 2.2 square miles (5.7 sq km) in area. Being uninhabited by humans, the rocky island is home to a unique ecosystem of plants and animals, including 39 species of birds. However, the island, and in fact the entire park, is largely inaccessible to the public.

Far more accessible is Theth National Park, which contains whole villages in the upper Shala River valley, near Shkoder. The nearly 6,500-acre (2,630 ha) park has some of the most extraordinary landscapes of the Albanian Alps, with high peaks and Grunas Canyon, a national monument. It's an important bird and plant area, and in 2017 it was designated as a Protected Historic Center.

The Grunas Waterfall cascades from a height of 98 feet (30 m) in Theth National Park.

INTERNET LINKS

https://www.un.org.al/what-we-do/environment-and-climate-change/environment-and-climate-change
This UN site provides an overview of Albania's environmental and climate challenges.

https://www.unece.org/fileadmin/DAM/env/epr/epr_studies/Synopsis/Albania_ECE.CEP.183_Synopsis.pdf
The executive summary of the 2018 UNECE environmental review is available in this document.

ALBANIANS

A boy wears a traditional Albanian folk costume as part of a music festival at Berat Castle.

7

A LBANIA HAS ONE OF THE MOST homogeneous populations in Europe, with ethnic Albanians making up nearly 83 percent of the population. Of the rest of the people living in Albania, almost 1 percent are Greek, and the rest are either Vlach (a group related culturally and linguistically to Romanians), Roma, Macedonian, Montenegrin, Egyptian, or unspecified.

Partly, this lack of diversity is the legacy of the more than four decades of extreme isolation the country endured under Enver Hoxha. Essentially, no one was allowed out of the country, and no one was allowed in.

Ethnic Albanians, as a people rather than as a nationality, make up the majority of the population of neighboring Kosovo. They are also found in significant numbers across the borders in other countries— southeastern Montenegro, western North Macedonia, southeastern Serbia, and northwestern Greece.

With migration, Albanians have spread across the globe, especially in Europe and the United States.

GHEGS AND TOSKS

Albanians trace their ancestry to the ancient Illyrian tribes that evolved into the Greek and Roman peoples. Documents from 14th-century

Albania has been losing population since the end of communism in 1991, when it reached 3.28 million. Large-scale emigration and lower fertility rates (the average number of children born to women during their reproductive years) are the main factors. An average fertility rate of 2.1 is usually required to keep a population stable. In 2020, Albania's rate was 1.53 children born per woman, and the population was predicted to fall to 2.66 million by 2050.

A young Albanian couple are dressed in traditional national attire.

travelers refer to a warlike people along the southeastern Adriatic coast who lived in tents that they packed up and moved as they needed to, rather than establishing fortified camps. One observer noted that they were superb archers and lancers. Families tended to be large, as clans sought to raise soldiers and workers who would replace those taken in war, forced into servitude, or killed in blood feuds.

Most of the people in Albania have historically fallen into two Albanian subgroups: northern Ghegs and southern Tosks. The Shkumbin River has traditionally divided the northern Ghegs from the southern Tosks. Though both groups speak the Albanian language of Shqip, their dialects differ.

The Ghegs are mountain people who even during Ottoman rule preserved a clan-oriented society. The clan was ruled by a tribal chief, but all were equal under his rule. A small minority of the Ghegs were Roman Catholic, but most were Sunni Muslim. Though they supported Albanian independence, their enthusiasm was tempered by a fear that a strong central government would erode tribal authority. This authority was codified in the Kanun, a 15th-century system of governance written by an Albanian chieftain named Leke Dukagjini. The Kanun was interpreted by the tribal chief, and its precepts even today form the basis of family and clan expectations, and thus of Albanian life.

The Tosks, living south of the Shkumbin River, have had more contact with people from outside the country because of their more accessible terrain. Though Tosks also were tribal people, the Ottoman influence was more strongly felt here. The Tosks were also primarily Muslim, but their community included Bektashi Muslims as well as Sunnis. The Bektashi Muslims, a small subset of Sufi Islam, were more tolerant of other religions and helped set a tolerant tone for Tosks, who also included in their numbers Eastern Orthodox Christians, who would later form the Albanian Orthodox Church.

Ghegs tend to be more animated than the Tosks, arguing loudly and appearing angry to outsiders. Traditionally, it is the Ghegs who supplied the armies with their soldiers and whose personalities and demeanor even today recall the fierce soldiers they once were. The Tosks, who were farmers, are generally seen as somewhat quieter and less boisterous.

A man herds goats in the mountainous north country of Fierze, Albania. The northern mountains were traditionally the home of the Gheg people.

THE ALBANIAN CHARACTER

At the time of Albanian independence in 1912, nearly 90 percent of the people were rural. Only three cities in Albania had more than 10,000 people, and the largest was Shkoder with 25,000. It was within the clans and rural communities that most people developed their sense of themselves as Albanians, and this self-image has not changed over the centuries.

People stroll along the pedestrian boulevard outside the Hotel Colosseo in Shkoder.

Adversity has shaped a character defined by loyalty and stoicism. Many Albanians have been raised by their parents to expect a war for each generation. In the face of such hardship, they remain generous and willing to share what they have with visitors or fellow Albanians in need.

Central to an Albanian's self-image is the concept of the *besa* (BEH-sah), or "word of honor." An Albanian proverb says, "An honest man will not break his word," and this is the cornerstone of the Albanian character. Besa confers the absolute certainty that what has been promised will be delivered. As part of the Kanun, besa survived the best efforts of the Turks and the communists to replace it with their own certainties. Besa regulated business transactions, marriage proposals, and all acts of faith between individuals and groups such as families and clans. With a population that was largely illiterate, besa was crucial to society at every level. Not only was it a matter of personal honor, but it was enforced by the group as well. Violating besa was punishable by death, and the shame and resulting consequences could extend to the whole family and beyond. The duty to avenge a violation of besa also applied to the extended family and was one of the causes of blood feuds extending for generations. Even today, Albanians are not likely to say they will do something they are not sure they can do.

Albanians are fervent handshakers. Visitors must shake hands with the host at the door and, once inside, with everyone present—beginning with the eldest and working down. Close friends may kiss on the cheek, but only with friends of the same gender. Once seated, the guest will be told, "You are welcome here," and will reply, "It is a pleasure to be here." On the street, Albanians shake hands every time they meet.

The communal nature of life under communism has led Albanians to expect less privacy and to offer less privacy than Westerners are accustomed to. A foreigner is of great interest to many Albanians, and they will not hesitate to interrupt a conversation among people they do not know.

JEWS

There used to be a comunnity of several hundred Jews in Albania. The story of this community during World War II is a tribute to the character of Albanians. Like other occupied countries in Europe, Albania was ordered by the fascists to round up and deport their Jewish citizens to extermination sites outside the country. Rather than comply, many Albanians sheltered their Jewish neighbors, hiding them in attics and barns until the end of the war, telling the Nazis that there were no Jews in Albania. Meanwhile, some Jews from other European countries found refuge in Albania, making it the only country on the continent to see an increase in its Jewish population during the war. In later years, nearly all of Albania's Jews emigrated to Israel. Only a handful remain in the country today.

ROMA

Roma, a people once popularly called Gypsies (the term is now considered offensive), are partly nomadic in Albania, as they are in many countries in

KOSOVO REFUGEES

Being one of the poorest nations in Europe, Albania has not attracted many economic immigrants. However, one unusual influx of people overwhelmed the country in the late 1990s. They sought safety and protection, not economic opportunities. Just as Albania was trying to recover from civil unrest following the disastrous pyramid scheme debacle in 1997, war erupted next door in Kosovo.

At the time, Kosovo was an autonomous province of Serbia, which itself was a part of the larger federation of Yugoslavia. Six Balkan republics together comprised Yugoslavia throughout much of the 20th century. Albania bordered three of them—the Kosovo part of Serbia, Macedonia, and Montenegro.

Unlike the rest of Serbia, Kosovo was made up largely of ethnic Albanians, and they wanted independence from Serbia. After the fall of communism in 1991, several Yugoslav nations declared independence, which set off a series of separate but related wars in the Balkans. Serbia had no intention of letting Kosovo break away, but Serbian Yugoslav leader Slobodan Milosevic did want to rid it of ethnic Albanians. To that end, he stripped Kosovo of its autonomy and initiated a policy of persecution of the Albanian Kosovars. The oppression escalated into "ethnic cleansing" massacres and other war crimes. The horrors sparked a mass exodus of people fleeing for their lives.

In the first half of 1999, as the Yugoslav army perpetrated more atrocities, NATO responded with air strikes against Yugoslav positions inside Kosovo. According to the UN High Commissioner for Refugees, more than 600,000 Albanians fled Kosovo seeking shelter in neighboring countries and beyond. Around 435,000 of them ended up in Albania, an enormous number for the small nation to absorb.

NATO, the United Nations, and several other organizations erected large refugee camps in Albania (shown below). There were serious food shortages. Support from international relief agencies was generous, but the crisis taxed an already unstable government.

Despite Albania's own precarious situation, the Albanians were welcoming to the refugees, sheltering many in their homes. After the hostilities ended a few months later, most of the refugees returned home. In 2008, Kosovo declared independence from Serbia. Today, it remains a partially recognized state, still in territorial dispute with Serbia.

Europe. Though they are officially said to make up less than 1 percent of the population, they are often undercounted. For example, the 2011 census counted 8,301 Roma people in Albania, but the European Roma Rights Center estimates the true number to be closer to 120,000.

The Roma tend to be secretive and keep very much to their own communities. They speak their own language, a Balkan variant of Romani, and many don't speak Albanian at all. In Albania, as in most European countries, those who are not nomadic usually live in poor conditions in settlements, lacking connections to basic infrastructure like water, electricity, and public services. Compared to other Albanians, they tend to be less educated and work in temporary manual labor. They are also subject to discrimination. Their children are commonly seen in the cities, begging for change from visitors.

In 2017, the government of Albania officially recognized the Roma as a national minority, a move that raises the level of their legal rights and protections. Among other things, it provides the children the right to be educated in their native language, which was previously not an option in public schooling.

INTERNET LINKS

https://balkaninsight.com/2019/11/14/the-clock-ticks-for-albanias -demographic-dividend
Albania's shrinking population is examined in this article.

https://www.timesofisrael.com/what-made-muslim-albanians-risk -their-lives-to-save-jews-from-the-holocaust
This article explains how the tradition of besa helped to save Jews in Albania during the Holocaust.

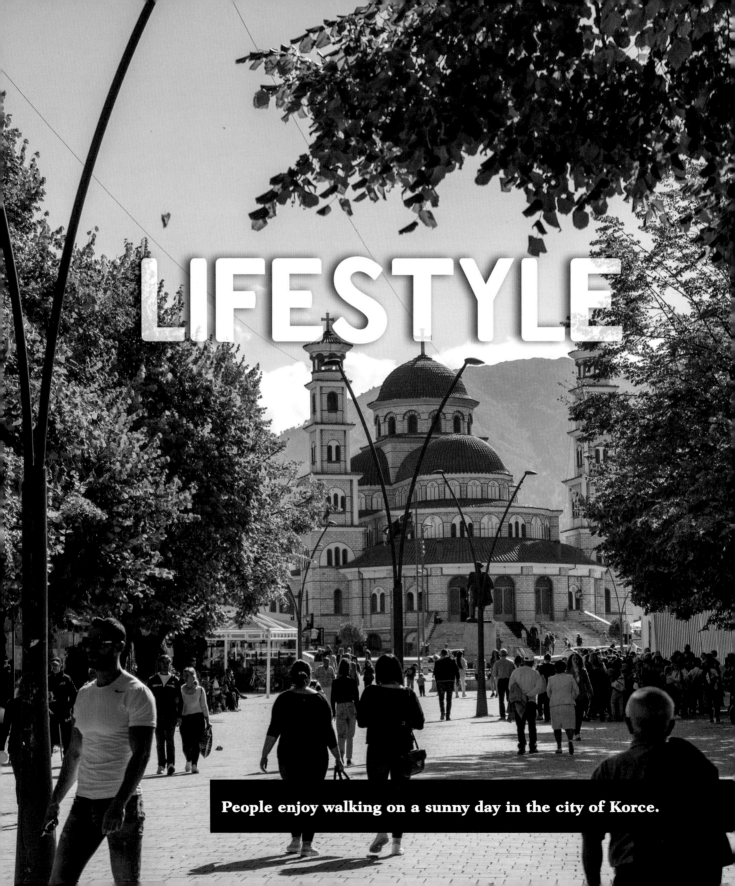

LIFESTYLE

People enjoy walking on a sunny day in the city of Korce.

ALBANIANS ARE PROUD OF BEING Albanian, even as they acknowledge the challenges their country faces in the 21st century. It is still in transition, looking to become a modern European nation after having been held back for 50 years in the isolation of totalitarian rule. However, Albanian culture has deep roots in the past, and old tribal values that might seem antiquated still hold great sway over the Albanian lifestyle. One of those is the traditional institution of the clan. In many ways, it still unofficially outranks the government as the legal authority of Albanian life.

In the mountain region of the north, the Gheg people historically owed their primary allegiance to kinship groups, and within those clans, to their families. Extended families—consisting of parents, their sons, their sons' wives and children, and their unmarried daughters—usually lived together. The family formed an independent residential and economic unit. Individual families could consist of as many as 60 members, who lived in small dwellings around the parents' larger home. The governing organization was the clan, and the clan leader settled disputes, arranged marriages, and determined the hierarchy within the group. Disputes that could not be settled by his intervention became blood feuds, which carried through to succeeding generations, sometimes to be continued in exile in other countries.

In the southern part of the country lived the Tosks. They were mostly Muslim, and the comparative accessibility of their terrain had left them less isolated and more open to outside influences. Though they, too, had tribal loyalties, these ties had been somewhat weakened by the feudal rule of the Turkish aristocracy. Their independence, like their isolation, was less complete.

Both Tosks and Ghegs recognized the complete authority of the father as head of the family (and this remains largely true today as well). Marriages were arranged in infancy, usually outside the clan. Failure to carry through on the arranged marriages could result in a blood feud. Upon the death of the father, the oldest son assumed leadership of the family, but the family's assets were divided among all the sons. Women were not allowed to own anything or to seek divorce.

Children were raised to respect their father and obey him without question. Any insult to the father might also result in a blood feud. Women were treated as servants and kept separate from the men.

Historically, Albanians have felt safe only inside their homes, and that feeling has not changed with the events of the last century. An Albanian home is generally clean and calm, with books, a computer, and a television, like many European homes. This is a great contrast, though, to the scene outside the home in many Albanian cities, where trash litters the streets, factories stand empty, and traffic is unregulated and terrifying. Though the country is in transition, the Albanian home remains the center of life. Sundays are reserved for the family, and guests who are invited to share that day with an Albanian family have been truly honored.

A DAY IN THE LIFE

In Muslim communities, women are expected to stay at home. Their lives are quite separate from those of the men. They usually rise early to make their family's breakfast. For the rest of the day, they clean and prepare the afternoon meal. It is a point of pride for Albanians that their homes are scrupulously clean.

Stronger than any written law in Albania is the ancient code of conduct known as the Kanun. It once ruled the country, and to a perhaps lesser extent, it still does. The social code comes from the extensive set of laws composed by a 15th-century Albanian nobleman, Leke Dukagjini. The rules were passed down orally over generations, only finally being published in the early 20th century. The Kanun is the source of the honor code of besa.

The Kanun also established the Albanian tradition of blood feuds. A blood feud, or gjakmarrja, is a dispute between two families or clans over a perceived matter of honor for which blood must be shed in revenge. The retaliation killing sets in motion an ongoing series of revenge murders that can continue over several generations, seemingly with no end. Entire families of someone who is targeted in a blood feud will hide in their homes for years. Children are pulled out of school and must stay indoors as well.

There are ways to break the cycle. Reconciliation can involve money payments and forgiveness. However, many Albanians regard forgiveness as shameful and cowardly.

Under the totalitarian rule of Enver Hoxha, the Kanun was strictly outlawed, but in the chaotic atmosphere that followed his death and the fall of communism, it was quickly revived. A lack of trust in the governmental justice system turned people back to the old ways.

In the early 1990s, the Albanian government initiated a large-scale reconciliation movement to

This tower in Theth was a place where an intended victim of a blood feud could stay safe.

end blood feuds and partially succeeded. However, the social unrest later in the decade stirred the ancient bloody pot once more, and some men turned again to gjakmarrja to settle scores. Although the old texts lay out specific rules, such as forbidding the murder of women and children, recent instances of blood vengeance appear to show little respect for or understanding of those rules. Even young children have been murdered.

Water may not be reliably available—though that situation is improving—so cleaning and preparing the afternoon meal, which is the main meal of the day, can be very labor intensive. Girls are expected to stay home as well, helping the women with the work of the house and learning how to take care of their own houses when they are grown.

After their breakfast, men begin their day at work. If they don't have jobs, they may spend much of their time strolling around town with their friends or sitting in the cafés drinking coffee or the Albanian national drink, raki, a Turkish liqueur. The Muslims of Albania identify themselves strongly as Muslim, but some do not observe the traditional prohibition on alcohol, so liquor is widely available. Boys are free to play with their friends or go to the cafés with the men. If classes are available, they will spend some time in school each day.

The evenings are often graced with visits. Friends and family drop in for a cup of Turkish coffee and to renew old acquaintances. Despite the availability of cell phones and the internet, this is how many Albanians keep in touch with each other and share the news of their lives. To visit is to confer honor on the

Men in Gjirokaster pass the time at a café.

host, so most visits are considered formal affairs, even within small groups, and the coffee is served in the best cups.

Hospitality is a virtue and a source of pride. Albanians will always pick up a check for their guest for coffee and drinks. Guests in the home will be offered food and drink, usually both coffee and raki, and will be expected to accept. Albanians even drink raki in the morning, as a breakfast beverage. Still, they are not heavy drinkers, and public drunkenness is a source of shame.

SAFETY AND SECURITY

Safety, security, and stability are complicated issues in Albania. On the one hand, everyday crime is relatively low. Visitors report generally feeling safe walking alone on the streets, especially in the daytime. In Tirana, the capital, the streets are as safe, or safer, than in many other European cities.

In fact, the homicide rate in Albania is less than half that of the United States. In 2017, for example, the homicide rate for Albania was 2.3 cases per 100,000 people. For the United States that year, the figure was 5.3. The rate of car theft in Albania in 2016 was 10.2 thefts per 100,000 people. That rate was down from a high of 23.2 in 2012. In the United States, however, the rate of car theft in 2016 was 236.9 per 100,000 people. (As an aside, it should be pointed out that while the official statistics for car theft in Albania are low, anecdotally the crime is said to be widespread.) Therefore, Albania appears to be a relatively safe place for the average person.

On the other hand, corruption and organized crime are very high, though they may not directly affect the safety of everyday life. For people involved in drug-related or other illegal activities, however, life may not be so safe. Albanian gangs linked to organized crime have a reputation for being particularly brutal.

In 2019, the US Department of State issued a travel advisory for the town of Lazarat in the south of Albania, due to potential violence associated with marijuana cultivation. Lazarat is well known as "the cannabis capital" of the country for its large-scale, but illegal, cultivation of marijuana. The local people are said to be heavily armed and will openly take on the police or even government soldiers.

With corruption heavily influencing the country's judiciary, people who have been victims of crime may not feel confident they will find justice. Accordingly, there is a culture of vigilantism, or taking the law into one's own hands, particularly regarding the traditional Kanun code of conduct.

EDUCATION

Public school is free and provided by the government. Schooling is mandatory for children in grades 1 through 9, and most students continue on into high school. The elementary school enrollment rate is very high, at about 96 percent, and the country's literacy rate is almost perfect, at about 98 percent. However, those figures change when applied to Albania's Roma children and disabled children, whose education is significantly disadvantaged.

There are other significant problems in Albania's education system. There is no state-subsidized preschool education. At least half the schools lack basic facilities, and around 25 percent of teachers are not qualified. Some textbooks are exceedingly shoddy and substandard, having been written by unqualified

Albanian children learn their numbers in a kindergarten class.

people. Not surprisingly, then, student achievement in Albania is among the lowest in Europe.

By European standards, Albania's education system is underfunded, with an average of 2.9 percent of GDP being spent on education. The EU average is 4.5 percent, and a 2017 UNICEF report on the underfunding of education in Albania stated that the government must increase its spending to a minimum of 5 percent of GDP on education in order to ensure the country's future economic growth.

HEALTH

In 2020, the average life expectancy at birth in Albania was 79 years, which is considered relatively good. That figure placed it at number 61 out of 228 countries, in which number 1 was the highest (Monaco, at 89.3 years) and 228 (Afghanistan, at 52.8 years) the lowest. Albania ranked not far behind the United States, at number 45, with a life expectancy that year of 80.3 years.

Albania has a universal health care system, and the constitution guarantees the right of citizens to that care. Nevertheless, the country has the lowest proportion of doctors for its population of any European nation. In 2016, there were 1.2 physicians per 1,000 people. For comparison: Neighbor Montenegro had 2.3, Croatia had 3.0, the United States had 2.6, and EU countries had an average of 3.6 doctors per 1,000 people. One reason for Albania's low rate of doctors is the so-called "brain drain." Qualified professionals often leave the country to find better-paying positions elsewhere. Albania's main medical school is the University of Medicine, formerly a department of the University of Tirana, and there are also nursing schools in other cities.

The country's health care is marred by substandard conditions in some hospitals. Another issue is a culture of doctors demanding additional off-the-record payments, an extension of the country's corruption problem.

Herbal medicine has a long history in Albania, and it is still practiced in the cities as well as in the villages and rural areas. Every city and town has a marketplace where people can buy the plants or prepared medicines they need.

In the countryside, people sometimes sell them at the roadside. Some of the plants widely available include Saint-John's-wort, wild chamomile, lungwort, heartsease, horse-chestnut seed, rue, and thorn apple. Many of these herbs are poisonous when taken in certain amounts or under certain circumstances, but the long, unbroken tradition of use generally keeps Albanians from making mistakes with them.

WOMEN

Traditionally, women in Albania have had two faces. One was the face of a beautiful creature lauded in legend and poetry. The other face was the mother and wife who bore, fed, and clothed her family and worked in the fields with her husband, maintaining the traditions and values handed down to her. As a free and strong spirit, the first face inspired dreams and art. The second face was restricted to the home, taking no part in the social or political lives of men.

Though the communist system that dominated Albania for over half a century brought repression and terror to the people, it also brought equality of opportunity and education. Women were paid equally for their work and held 30 percent of government positions. Girls, as well as boys, were given at least eight years of education and equal opportunities for advanced education and training. Women soon became more productive than men and accounted for 80 percent of the light industrial workers and those working in the field of education.

After the fall of communism in 1991, most of those women became unemployed. The number of women in government and in professions such as law and medicine fell dramatically, and many women have again become restricted to a life in the home. In the rural areas, women once again work the land, which has been privatized and divided into smallholdings. Their work is especially arduous, since the equipment is outdated, worn-out, or nonexistent. Many of the men have emigrated in search of employment, leaving the women to do their work as well.

The equality bestowed under communism had shallow roots and no tradition behind it. Today, religious tradition has taken its place, and women no longer compete on equal footing. Some have organized and tried to assert themselves in favor of social change and equality, but in an economy with mass unemployment, job equality is a small prize.

VIOLENCE AGAINST WOMEN   Albania's entrenched culture of patriarchal authority, with its code of honor and shame, strict gender roles, and gender inequality, contributes to the problem of domestic violence. In 2013, a survey by Albania's Institute of Statistics found that 59.4 percent of Albanian women reported experiencing domestic violence at some point during their lives. However, the topic is not openly discussed much in the country and is considered a family's private business. As such, acts of violence against women are most likely underreported.

INTERNET LINKS

https://www.aljazeera.com/indepth/features/2016/03/albania -dark-shadow-tradition-blood-feuds-160318033023140.html
This article describes life for people trapped in traditional blood feuds.

https://balkaninsight.com/2019/09/03/tradition-denies-albanian -women-right-to-property
The topic of this article is how the Albanian Kanun tradition creates a wide gender gap in wealth.

http://www.instat.gov.al/en
Albania's Institute of Statistics (INSTAT) provides reports and statistics on health, gender, crime, and other lifestyle topics.

https://www.vqronline.org/reporting-articles/2017/10/land -vendettas-go-forever?src=longreads
This in-depth article offers a broad and fascinating view of Albanian life under the code of Kanun.

RELIGION

A statue of Mother Teresa stands in the center of Shkoder.

8

FOR HUNDREDS OF YEARS, ALBANIA was a country that tolerated a multiplicity of religions—Christianity, Islam, and Judaism. In 1967, it declared atheism its national "religion" and outlawed and repressed any other religious practice. Mosques and churches were closed.

Then, in 1990, in the midst of many other changes, Albania began allowing private religious practice once again. In the 2011 census, only 2.5 percent of Albanians claimed to be atheists, though another 16.2 percent did not specify a religion. Meanwhile, 56.7 percent identified as Muslim; 10 percent as Roman Catholic; 6.8 percent as Orthodox Christian; 2.1 percent as Bektashi, a Sufi Muslim sect; and 5.7 percent as other.

Scholars estimate that in the first half of the 20th century, roughly 70 percent of the people were Muslim, 20 percent Orthodox Christian, and 10 percent Roman Catholic. However, with religion having been repressed for almost 50 years and outlawed for nearly 25 of them, many people at the end of the century had no tradition at all of a theistic belief.

ATHEISM

When Enver Hoxha outlawed religion in 1967, he destroyed or repurposed 2,169 mosques, monasteries, and churches. Those that were not destroyed outright were converted into storage places, sports arenas, and even public bathrooms. A law prohibiting religious practices prescribed long

Although the woman known worldwide as Mother Teresa was not an Albanian national, the country nevertheless claims her as one of its own. That's because she was of ethnic Albanian heritage, born in Macedonia to ethnic Albanian parents. In 2016, the Roman Catholic nun was canonized (declared a saint) by Pope Francis.

The medieval Byzantine Church of the Holy Trinity stands on a hill above the old city of Berat.

prison sentences for those who transgressed and public execution for those who tried to leave the country. Every religious and cultural value connected with the past was erased from public consciousness. Religious scholars and leaders were imprisoned, executed, or forced to renounce their beliefs.

A whole generation grew up without faith, without seeing a mosque or a church. Worshipping privately was also dangerous because secret police were everywhere and neighbors were obliged to spy on each other. Schoolteachers even interrogated young children for signs of illegal religious activities being carried on at home. Yet religion remained deep in the hearts of some of the people. Islamic ceremonies were organized in secret. The faithful fasted during the holy Ramadan month without calling attention to themselves. Likewise, Christians held secret communion services and privately familiarized themselves with Bible stories.

THE "RELIGION" OF ALBANIANISM

In 1878, the Albanian writer Pashko Vasa, a Catholic, wrote his famous poem "Oh Albania." The poem calls upon the Albanian people to overcome religious divisions through a united sense of themselves as a people—a concept Vasa called Albanianism. The poem laments that Albanians' lack of unity had allowed the beloved motherland to be taken over by foreigners (the Ottoman Empire). In one of the final stanzas of the poem, Vasa says, "Feja e shqyptarit asht shqyptarija" ("The faith of the Albanian is Albanianism"). This phrase became a slogan for Albanian nationalists, and in the 20th century, the dictator Enver Hoxha used it as a justification for outlawing religion itself. The only religion of the Albanians, Hoxha insisted, was Albanianism.

O moj Shqypni (condensed from "Oh Albania")
By Pashko Vasa

Oh Albania, poor Albania,
Who has shoved your head in the ashes?
Once you were a great lady,
The men of the world called you mother ...
But today, Albania, tell me, how are you
  faring now?
Like an oak tree, felled to the ground!
The world walks over you, tramples
  you underfoot,
And no one has a kind word for you.
Like the snow-covered mountains, like
  blooming fields
You were clothed, today you are in rags.
Neither your reputation nor your
  oaths remain,
You yourself have destroyed them in your
  own misfortune.
Albanians, you are killing your brothers,
Into a hundred factions you are divided,

Some say "I believe in God," others "I in
  Allah,"
Some say "I am Turk," others "I am Latin,"
Some "I am Greek," others "I am Slav,"
But you are brothers, all of you, my
  hapless people!
The priests and the hodjas have*
  deceived you
To divide you and keep you poor ...
Who has the heart to let her die,
Once such a heroine, and today so weak?
This beloved mother, are we to
  abandon her
To be trampled underfoot by the
  foreigners? ...
Wake, Albanian, from your slumber,
Let us, brothers, swear in common
And not look to church or mosque,
The Albanian's faith is Albanianism!

*Muslim schoolmasters

Albanian religious practices have a pragmatic side that reflects the history of believers in a hostile atmosphere. Since religious practice was illegal and therefore very dangerous, Muslims minimized the outward manifestations of their beliefs. As a result, many Muslims in Albania today do not observe the dietary laws or the requirements that they pray five times a day.

This tradition of accommodating the enemy for the sake of survival has a Christian equivalent as well. During the Turkish occupation, Christianity was tolerated in an otherwise Muslim land. However, Christians were required to surrender one of their sons for military duty and to pay taxes that were not demanded of Muslims. To save their sons and their money, many Christians converted to Islam, and others pretended to convert, practicing their own faith in secret.

After communism fell, the old mosques and churches were reopened as places of worship. Those destroyed were rebuilt or replaced as money allowed. The Albanian Muslim community took shape and coalesced around its spiritual leader, Hafiz Sabri Koci Effendi, who emerged after languishing in communist prisons for 25 years.

ISLAM

Today, Islam in Albania is thriving. However, many of its followers point to their faith as a "European-style" Islam, one that fits comfortably with Western culture. For the most part, women wear Western clothing, and the religious culture is not as strict as in the Middle East. There is some concern that poverty might cause some Albanian Muslims to radicalize, and there are small factions, supported by the Saudis, for example, that are trying to institute a much more militant version of Islam there. Inevitably, at least so far, though, such attempts have mostly run up against the people's stronger sense of themselves as Albanians first.

Like Muslims everywhere, Albanians follow the teachings of the Quran, the writings of Muhammad. They believe that Muhammad was the prophet of God. Beyond that belief, though, Albanians remain quite independent in their beliefs and practices. As a group, Albanian Muslims, both in and outside the country, resist a tendency toward the fundamentalism of countries such as Saudi Arabia

and parts of Iraq. Having lived under the most rigorous totalitarianism in which both democracy and religion were banned, they are inclined to value both their religious heritage and a democratic government.

Nor are Albanians likely to allow foreigners to tell them that their customs must be abandoned and their behavior determined by Islamic totalitarians. With an isolated culture, a language without close relatives, and a tradition of avoiding religious differences in the interest of national unity, Albanians are generally wary of outsiders trying to lead them. They believe in the validity of their own history, their own culture, and their own Albanian model of Islam based on interfaith respect and the understanding that religion is private. This means that as Muslims, they love both Allah and their neighbors.

The Great Mosque of Tirana, the largest mosque in in the Balkans, was built by Turkey and completed in 2020. Not all Albanians are happy about the grandiose new building, including many Muslims, because of its Ottoman style and a general distrust of Turkey.

The Resurrection of Christ Orthodox Cathedral, built in 1995, is the main Orthodox church in Korce.

CHRISTIANITY

Christianity has had followers in Albania since the fourth century CE. When Christianity split into the Roman Catholic and Eastern Orthodox branches, Catholicism was dominant among the northern Ghegs, while Orthodoxy was dominant among the southern Tosks—although Muslims made up a majority of both groups. Today, around 10 percent of Albanians are Roman Catholics, still mostly in the northern part of the country. In Lezhe County, they make up more than 72 percent of the population, and in neighboring Shkoder County, the northernmost part of Albania, they account for 47 percent.

The other main Christian church in Albania is the Eastern Orthodox Church. Both Roman Catholics and Orthodox Christians believe in one God, as expressed through the Trinity—the Father, the Son, and the Holy Spirit or Holy Ghost.

They both believe in the divinity of Jesus Christ. Both churches started out as one, but split in 1054 over theological differences. Since then, the church cultures have grown further apart. For example, the church services and traditions are quite different. Unlike the Catholic Church, which is headed by the pope in Rome, the Eastern Orthodox churches are guided by the patriarch of Constantinople (Istanbul, Turkey), but they operate with more independence. The Albanian Orthodox Church was established in 1922.

The savage repression of religion from 1949 to 1990 left the Albanian Orthodox Church without leaders. All the bishops had been killed or had died in prison or in exile. Since then, more than 250 churches have been rebuilt or restored, and more than 100 clergy have been ordained. Today, it claims a membership of 500,000. However, the 2011 census pointed to a membership of about 205,000.

INTERNET LINKS

http://www.albanianliterature.net/authors/classical/vasa/index.html
The life of the Albanian poet Pashko Vasa is described on this page.

https://www.newsweek.com/2015/04/03/hardliners-nightmare-religious-tolerance-europes-only-majority-muslim-country-318212.html
The state of religion in today's Albania is explored in this article.

https://pulitzercenter.org/reporting/albania-gets-religion
This 2019 article discusses the resurgence of religion in Albania.

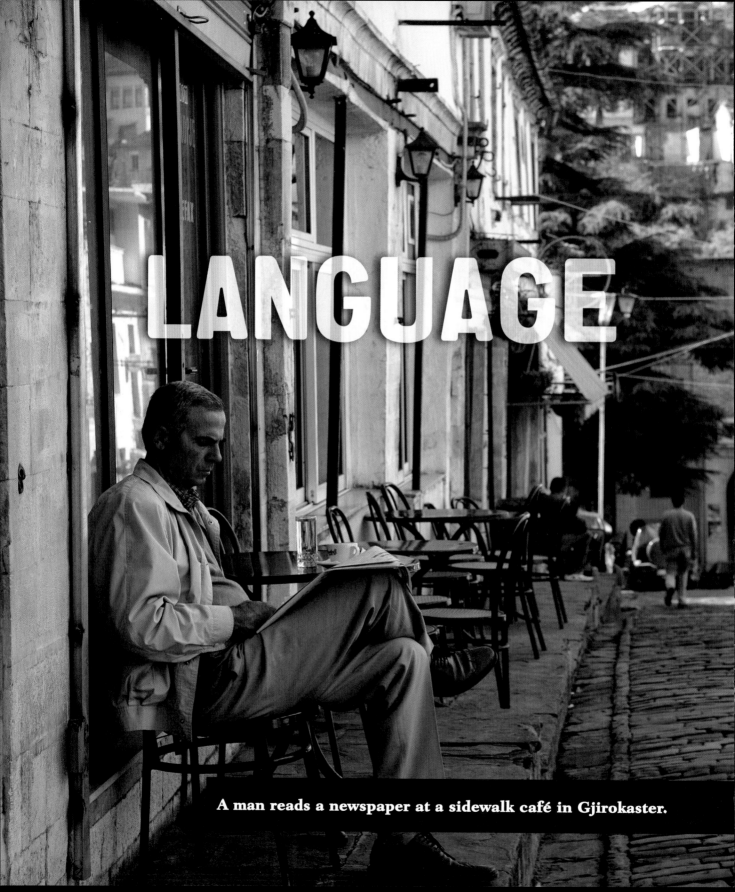

LANGUAGE

A man reads a newspaper at a sidewalk café in Gjirokaster.

9

NO ONE IS QUITE SURE WHERE THE Albanian language came from. It's sort of a lonely language, in that it comprises its own branch of the Indo-European languages. It's unique and unrelated to any other language known today.

Albanians call their language Shqip. They call themselves Shqiptaret (Albanians); the singular—an Albanian—is Shqiptar; and their country, Albania, is Shqiperi. Shqip is spoken by about 7.6 million people throughout Albania, its neighboring countries, and the lands to which Albanians have relocated.

In Albania, the language has two main dialects, Gheg and Tosk. Like the people of the same name, Gheg is spoken mainly in the north, as well as in Montenegro, Kosovo, Serbia, North Macedonia, and Bulgaria. Tosk, which is the official language of Albania, is spoken in the southern part of the country, as well as in Turkey, Greece, and Italy. However, there are intermediate, transitional variations of the two dialects in central Albania, and speakers of the two dialects generally have no trouble understanding each other.

ANCIENT ORIGINS?

The origins of Shqip are unknown, but many scholars think it might derive from an ancient Illyrian language spoken in Albania over 2,000 years ago. Others surmise that it might have arisen from some other now-extinct language, perhaps Thracian or Dracian, from the Balkan region.

However, not enough is known about the extinct languages to make the necessary connections.

The earliest references to an Albanian language come from travelers from other lands in the 14th century. These travelers noted that the language was different from the Greek, Latin, and Slavic tongues spoken throughout the area and that none of the speakers of those languages could understand Albanian. Although the language seems to have been well established by then, no written examples of it remain.

MESHARI

The earliest known book written in Shqip is a religious book called *Meshari*, meaning missal, by Gjon Buzuku, a Catholic cleric, probably from northern Albania. The Vatican Library has the only known existing copy of the book, originally a 188-page volume, with many illustrations and illuminated letters. The first 16 pages and the frontispiece are missing, so its exact date of publication is unknown, but it is believed to be from 1555. Today, a publishing house in Prishtina, Kosovo, is named after Gjon Buzuku.

Meshari has been valuable to scholars and historians because so much of its text is familiar. It consists largely of translations of texts that are known from other contexts, such as the New Testament of the Bible and Catholic liturgical prayers and rituals. The language patterns of the text have much to tell about Shqip as it existed during the time the book was written.

ALPHABET SOUP

Throughout the centuries of Turkish domination, the Albanians maintained their spoken language. In the 19th century, they even began to publish books in Albanian, though the alphabet was not yet codified, and to teach their children in Albanian-language schools. They persisted in their use of Shqip both within and outside Albania, despite opposition from the Turks, as well as from Greece, Serbia, and Montenegro.

The Albanian alphabet is based on the Latin alphabet, with several additional letters to accommodate some uniquely Shqip sounds. It consists of 36 letters.

Not all of them have English sound equivalents, the closest being Spanish or French. The Albanian alphabet as it exists today took some time to evolve and coalesce. In 1824, Naum Veqilharxhi developed an alphabet he called Evetor in an effort to free the language of Greek and Latin influences. Other alphabets in use at the time included Arabic- and Greek-influenced versions, and one called Istanbul. Several literary societies developed their own alphabets as well.

By the 20th century, it was becoming clear that a country as tiny as Albania was not well served by upward of 10 alphabets, and so in 1908, the Alphabet Congress was convened. For the next three years, controversy prevented settling on just one alphabet. Catholics felt their teachings could only be rendered in a Latin-based alphabet, while a group called the Young Turks maintained that a non-Arabic alphabet violated Islamic law. In cities throughout the country, people demonstrated in favor of their alphabetic choice. In 1911, the Young Turks, who had been told by their clerics that they would be considered infidels if they used the Latin alphabet, nevertheless dropped their objections, and the script used today was adopted. It is called Bashkimi, meaning "union," and is named after the literary society that developed it.

A bookstore displays its wares in the center of Shkoder.

COMMUNICATING IN ALBANIA

Telephone communication in Albania barely existed before 1990. Political restrictions forbade international calls, and poverty and technological backwardness prevented domestic calls. In 1990, only 1 in 100 Albanians had a phone. With the overthrow of the communist government, progress in telephone communication was expected, but civil unrest throughout the 1990s resulted in an actual decline, as people in the countryside tore down and used the telephone poles to build fences. The telephone lines in Albania are

In Shqip, the letters B, D, F, H, K, L, M, N, P, R, S, T, V, and Z make the same sounds they do in English. (Notice there is no W in this alphabet.) The other letters make the following sounds:

Letter	Sound	Letter	Sound
A	like a *in opera*	NJ	like first n *in onion*
C	like ts *in curtsy*	O	like o *in opera*
Ç	like ch *in church*	Q	like ch *in chair*
DH	like th *in this*	RR	a rolled r
E	like e *in tell*	SH	like sh *in shun*
Ë	like u *in bug*	TH	like th *in think*
G	like g *in gun*	U	like oo *in doom*
GJ	like j *in jam*	X	like ds *in beds*
I	like i *in is, or like* ee *in sheep*	XH	like j *in jungle*
J	like y *in yellow*	Y	like y *in yew*
LL	like ll *in tell*	ZH	like s *in vision*

outdated and damaged, but cellular phones have improved access for people throughout the country. Very few people have landlines, but by now almost everyone has a cell phone.

Albania has more than 65 TV stations, including several that broadcast nationally. Albanian TV broadcasts are also available to Albanian-speaking populations in neighboring countries. In addition, many viewers have access to Italian and Greek TV broadcasts via terrestrial reception. Cable TV is available to those who can afford it. Albania has begun a government-mandated conversion from analog to digital broadcast, and the government has pledged to provide analog-to-digital converters to low-income families affected by this decision. There are 2 public radio networks and about 80 private radio stations.

The internet is gaining in popularity. There was a 66.4 percent user rate in 2016, which has no doubt grown in the years since. Relatively few people people—12 per 100—have fixed broadband services. However, 1.3 million Albanians used mobile broadband services in 2019.

GESTURES AND CONVERSATIONS

Gestures are an important way of communicating in any culture, and in Albania, Westerners have some adjustments to make. People say no by nodding their heads. Yes is signified by shaking their heads from side to side. With foreigners, Albanians are reluctant to express disagreement, and they will sometimes listen without expression rather than disagree. Among themselves, however, they often argue boisterously.

MANY LANGUAGES

Albanians take pride in the uniqueness of their language and in its reputation for difficulty. Still, visitors don't usually have trouble communicating because so many Albanians speak more than one language. Some speak English, mostly younger people who may speak three or four languages. The most widely spoken foreign language is Italian because of the Italian TV stations that have been widely accessible since the years of communism. In the south of the country, many people speak Greek, and along the Serbian border some speak Serbo-Croatian. Older Albanians may have learned Russian in the days of Albania's alliance with the Soviet Union, but they probably haven't had good reason to speak it for many years. During the 1950s, while Albania and China enjoyed good relations, people who are now older citizens studied in China under cultural exchange programs. Today, after a long absence, these programs have resumed, and young Albanians are once again studying in China and learning Chinese.

INTERNET LINKS

https://www.britannica.com/topic/Albanian-language
Encyclopedia Britannica offers an overview of the Albanian language.

https://www.omniglot.com/writing/albanian.htm
This language site offers an introduction to Shqip.

ARTS

A craftsman carves stone in the
traditional way in Gjirokaster.

10

I N ALBANIA, STORYTELLING IS AS OLD as time. Albanians have a rich tradition of folktales and legends that were passed on through the generations over centuries. Even today, the old stories are told in the rural areas, in the evenings in front of a fire, perhaps. Like folktales the world over, Albanian stories center on the struggle between the forces of good and evil, but their influences reflect Albania's history of invasion and occupation.

The oldest Albanian epics featured heroic noblemen, fairies, and gods. Stories that originated during the Turkish occupation tell of resistance and freedom fighters. These stories were written down for the first time in the 1950s. Until then, they existed in the oral tradition, part song and part tale, performed at community ceremonies and family gatherings. In earlier times, they were performed by traveling singer-poets who were welcomed into the communities as wise and accomplished men.

In addition to preserving the heroic tales, Albanian epics also reinforced traditional values such as the sanctity of the tribe and family, the importance of the promise, and the necessity of the blood feud in the defense of honor and family. These are values that to this day define Albanians, some of whom can recite in detail wrongs done to their families in the two world wars.

Handwoven carpets, leather goods, silver and copper ware, stone carving, and many other crafts are part of Albania's heritage. The number of craftspeople with the skills to create traditional goods has been shrinking. Such artisans are in danger of becoming extinct. Crafts fairs, such as the one at the National Folklore Festival of Gjirokaster, are helping to encourage a new generation to learn these skills.

LITERATURE

The purges of intellectuals in Albania after World War II nearly brought to a halt any new literature and much consideration of the literature of the past. However, in 1961, after Albania broke off ties with the Soviet Union, a revived Albanian nationalism gave rise to a desire among the people for artistic expression. Though the government permitted only works of social realism that celebrated the communist cause and its values, artists were able, as they often are in totalitarian states, to express themselves obliquely, in subtle ways.

Albanian writer Ismail Kadare is pictured in Milan, Italy, in 2018.

ISMAIL KADARE Author Ismail Kadare, born in 1936, grew to maturity under communism. In 1963, he published his first major novel in French. *The General of the Dead Army* brought him great acclaim in Albania and internationally. He continued to write in both French and Albanian. Most of his novels have since been translated into English, including *Chronicle in Stone* (1987), *Broken April* (1990), and *The Palace of Dreams* (1993).

Kadare was regarded not only as a great writer and intellectual, but also as a voice against totalitarianism, which naturally brought him into conflict with the Albanian government. Kadare's artistic and intellectual restlessness brought to the forefront the complexity of life under tyranny. He has maintained that an "inner freedom" is of primary artistic importance and can thrive under the worst political circumstances. (Today, some critics accuse him of having a "Eurocentric," anti-Muslim perspective.)

By 1990, Kadare's work had caused enough displeasure among the authorities that he could no longer work and live with any degree of safety within Albania. Just months before the collapse of the regime, he fled to France, where he was granted political asylum. Since the fall of communism, he has maintained a dual citizenship, spending time in both countries. He has won many of literature's top international prizes, and in 2016, he was deemed a Commander of the Legion of Honor by his adopted nation. (The Legion of Honor is France's highest award and is bestowed by the president.)

MUSINE KOKALARI   The potential masterpiece that Albania's first major female writer might have produced will never be known. The story of Musine Kokalari is a sad one, but it's a tale that parallels that of Albania itself. Born in Turkey in 1917 to Albanian parents, she returned with them to Albania as a young child. Her family owned a bookstore, and she went on to study literature in Rome. It was there that she decided to become a writer. It was also in Rome that she developed strong anti-fascist political feelings, which she brought back to Albania.

She wrote in the Gjirokastrian dialect of her hometown and produced a collection of homespun stories called *As My Old Mother Tells Me* (1941). Today, that collection is considered the first female-written literary work in the history of Albania (presumably meaning the first to acquire any public recognition). Later, she published two more books. By 1945, as World War II was ending, she was running her own bookstore and joined the Albanian League of Writers. She became active in politics, published articles in which she spoke out against fascism, and demanded justice for the communists' execution of her brothers. She was arrested, tried, and sentenced to prison, where she was tortured, and eventually she was sentenced to hard labor. She was forbidden to write, but she nevertheless wrote a manuscript in secret about how she helped to found the Social Democratic Party.

In 1983, Kokalari died in prison, in complete isolation, after being refused medical treatment for cancer. In 1993, she was posthumously declared a Martyr of Democracy by Sali Berisha, the president of Albania. Today, a school in Tirana bears her name, and a 2017 Albanian postage stamp was issued in her honor.

VISUAL ARTS

The visual arts in Albania have for centuries been a reflection of the ethnic and religious culture of its people.

Early Illyrians left tiny metal figurines and pottery that recent archaeological digs have retrieved. These and other artifacts show the Illyrians to have been skilled metalworkers and potters, as well as stonecutters, leatherworkers, and weavers. Medieval painters and metalworkers produced icons of exceptional beauty. The city of Elbasan recorded over 45 craft guilds in the 17th century, where trained artisans produced leather goods, textiles, jewelry, and silver goods to export throughout the Ottoman Empire.

The 16th-century painter Onufri is one of Albania's most celebrated artists. He was a painter of icons, the sacred art of the Orthodox Christian Church. His icons show his skill as a master dyemaker as well as painter. His representational skill and use of color are equally deft. Some of Onufri's icons are embellished with hammered gold filigree.

Kole Idromeno is perhaps the most famous of the painters in the realist style. He is often said to have been the artist who introduced realism to Albania.

The communist government was more inclined to put its people to work on farms and in factories than in artist collectives, but statuary was a notable exception. Throughout Albania, statues of Enver Hoxha and other communist leaders were ubiquitous. Since the fall of communism, they have been preserved in museums but are no longer visible anywhere else.

Since 1990, the freedom to work in any medium and to represent any subject has resulted in a rebirth of painting and a move into multimedia art. Young artists working in Albania show their work at fairs and festivals—and increasingly, on the internet.

The mosaic on the facade of the National History Museum in Tirana features the heroic, propagandistic style of art that was typical of the communist era.

FILM

The painter and photographer Kole Idromeno presented the first Albanian-produced films in Shkoder in 1909. Over the years that followed, foreign films were commonly shown in movie theaters in the bigger cities. Albania developed its own filmmaking industry, and the first studio was founded in 1952. Under communism, films served ideological purposes—that is, they glorified the values and stories that the government wanted the people to see. Still, filmmakers did what they could within the restrictions of propaganda, and some managed to create works of quality.

However, because Albania was so politically and culturally isolated from the rest of the world between the 1960s and the 1980s, filmmakers lost touch with contemporary international cinema. Their works became stodgy and insular, unable to embrace artistic change and creative exploration. Indeed, the government suppressed any such notions.

That Albania even developed a film industry is surprising considering the lack of money available for what might have been considered a luxury. In addition, people who worked on the technical side were trained on obsolete Russian and Chinese equipment, and there were no film schools in the country.

Since the fall of communism, as with so much else, there came a resurgence of artistic engagement in film. Albanian filmmakers reached out to French film studios—and some in other countries as well—for partnerships in funding, training, technical support, and equipment. Soon, Albanians started making award-winning films. One, called *Slogans*, was released in 2001. The production of that film illustrates how international cooperation can keep a small industry alive under difficult conditions. The movie, like many Albanian films, was based on a novel. *The Stone Slogans* by Ylljet Alicka had been published in France as well as in Albania, so it had some international regard. Because there were no film schools in Albania at the time, the novelist worked with a Belgian screenwriter, Yves Hanchar, to transform the novel into a screenplay. After the film was made, with French technical assistance and money, the French producers distributed the movie in France, while the Albanian producers distributed it in Albania. *Slogans* became the first Albanian film to be shown at the prestigious Cannes Film Festival in France.

Since then, Albania has produced many high-quality movies. *The Forgiveness of Blood* (2011) is about the consequences of a blood feud for a family in a remote area of modern-day Albania. *Daybreak* (2017) tells the story of a young woman and her infant son trying to stay afloat in hard times. *The Delegation* (2018) takes place in 1990 when Western diplomats arrive in Albania to investigate human rights abuses under the communist regime.

In 1997, the Albanian Center of Cinematography was founded to support and encourage filmmakers in the country. It helps to develop international co-productions, which helps improve a film's chances for a wider distribution.

MUSIC

The isolation of Albanians, especially in the mountains, had the fortunate effect of preserving traditions in dance and music for centuries. Until after World War II, in fact, traditional music was the only music Albanians knew. Under communism, much of that music was recorded and preserved in archives. At the same time, the government introduced the people to Western music and trained classical musicians. Today, with open borders, mass media, and the internet, Albanians are exposed to a richness of music—traditional, classical, and all of today's popular styles.

Local music was probably once used to accompany the rituals of the Illyrian tribes. At that time, the music consisted of a simple melodic line accompanied by drums, chorus, primitive wind instruments made of wood or reed, and maybe a harp.

Despite 500 years of Turkish occupation, Albanians maintained an identity of their own that extends to their musical styles to this day. Though influenced by their occupiers, their music has been that of the Albanian folk, not the Turks. Up until around 1945, the only Albanian music that existed had been preserved through the oral folk tradition, as no system of notation or recording had been developed.

REGIONAL DIFFERENCES   As in all things Albanian, isolation made the music of the Ghegs in the north and the Tosks in the south sound very different.

The music of the Tosks, in fact, sounds different from just about any other music. The Tosk traditional polyphonic singing, or part-singing, sounds to the untrained ear as if all the singers are performing different songs that start at a variety of times and proceed to a variety of finishes. This type of music is not unknown in Europe, but it dates back to the earliest forms of polyphonic music and is not heard elsewhere today.

The Ghegs, in contrast, have a mostly monophonic folk tradition, which is more familiar to people in the West. In the north, the songs are usually sung by one person, and the theme is a heroic endeavor, most often against the Turks. Music in the south of Albania is more communal, often with a chorus. Songs and poems tend to be more lyrical or contemplative than narrative.

Teen boys in Albanian costume play folk music on a traditional flute and a *lahuta*.

Albanian music, both instrumental and vocal, features a technique sometimes called gradual pitch blend, which differs from the Western practice of hitting a note precisely on its pitch. Applying this technique to jazz and newer musical forms is now considered innovative.

TRADITIONAL INSTRUMENTS   As in most folk music, old-style traditional instruments often accompany Albanian singing and folk dancing. The most common instrument is the flute, but bagpipes and drums are also heard at many informal gatherings. One instrument, the *lahuta* (LAH-hoo-tah), is a stringed instrument much like the lute that was common in northern Europe during the Renaissance. It is one of the oldest instruments still in use in Europe. The oral poets played the lahuta to call the people to hear their recitations.

In the second half of the 20th century, the Institute of Popular Culture in Tirana collected traditional songs, dances, and poetry. Today, it has a collection of about 1 million verses, 40,000 proverbs, and nearly 10,000 recordings.

A young couple in Albanian costume perform a traditional courtship dance in Lepushe.

FOLK DANCES AND COSTUMES

Folk music is intricately connected to traditional dance and costumes. All three together create an art form of great color, energy, and drama. Dances often reference historic tales—men's dances, for example, will show off the warriors' strength, courage, and skills.

At weddings and music and dance festivals, Albanians welcome the opportunity to wear the costumes that represent their traditional garb. As recently as 1940, these were not costumes at all for many, but daily dress. Though the country is tiny, the costumes are varied and unique to each location. Like the music, the costumes reflect the influence of Albania's mixed cultures, brought in by the invaders.

BERAT AND GJIROKASTER

Two historic city centers in southern-central Albania together comprise one of the country's UNESCO World Heritage sites. The Historic Centers of Berat and Gjirokaster show rare examples of an architectural style typical of the Ottoman period.

Berat (right), which dates to the 6th century BCE, has a fortified center with medieval Byzantine churches and mosques decorated with elaborate murals and frescoes. At the top of the city's distinctive rocky hill sits Berat Castle, also known as the Kala. Its foundations date to the 4th century BCE, but the fortress was built mostly in the 13th century. In the 1700s, Berat was famous for its crafts guilds—including leather workers, metal workers, silversmiths, and silk makers. Today, it is a cultural center.

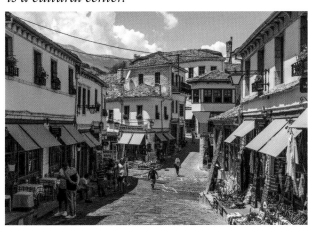

Gjirokaster (left), in the Drinos River valley, features a series of distinctive two-story houses which were developed in the 17th century. The town also has a historic bazaar, an 18th-century mosque, and two churches of the same period. Like Berat, the town sits below an ancient castle, Gjirokaster Fortress, which hosts the Gjirokaster National Folklore Festival every five years.

Gjirokaster was the birthplace of the Albanian dictator Enver Hoxha and the novelist Ismail Kadare, and home to the persecuted writer Musine Kokalari.

Folk costumes are offered for sale as souvenirs at a market in Tirana.

In the city of Tropoje, for example, men dress in a close-fitting white skullcap and loose white shirt. A short vest, black in front and red in the back, goes over the shirt. Low-slung black trousers are held up by a complex series of sashes, one white, the others colored and elaborately fringed. Women also wear a snowy white shirt topped with a short vest. A long white skirt with a bright red apron completes the outfit.

In Tirana, the white skullcap is still the first identifying mark of the Albanian man. Like his countrymen to the north, he wears a white shirt and black pants. His vest, though, is heavily embroidered and distinctive. The woman's vest also is uniquely decorated, often with the same motifs and colors as the man's. She may wear a small hat that coordinates with her vest, or she may have her head completely covered in the Muslim tradition by a shawl. Her long white skirt will be covered in front by a large, beautifully embroidered apron, and her long-sleeved blouse will proclaim the artistry of her mother or herself in a color and design that are her family's alone.

In southern Albania, the man's white skullcap is slightly larger, more like a Turkish fez, but still identifiably Albanian. The white shirt is still there as well, as is the short vest. Instead of the black trousers, the man wears a white skirt over tight white pants or leggings. Women wear bright, embroidered skirts, aprons, and vests. In Dropull, women may wear a headpiece composed of a lacy, white, tiara-shaped hat and a shoulder-length veil. Their white skirts and blouses are topped with one-piece embroidered aprons that cover both their blouse fronts and their skirts.

The elements of the Albanian costume have symbolic meaning. The black vest, the *xhokia e zeze* (joh-KEE-ah eh ZEH-zeh), for example, represents the mourning of the Albanian people for the death of Skanderbeg, their national hero. Various forms of men's trousers can indicate vassalage under tyranny. When dancers and singers wear their costumes, they add a visual significance to their performance that goes beyond their music and movements.

INTERNET LINKS

https://www.albanian-folklore.com/dances
This folklore site focuses on traditional dances.

https://www.albanianinstitute.org
The Albanian Institute in New York showcases a broad range of Albanian arts and culture.

http://www.albanianliterature.net
This site provides many folktales and legends in English, as well as information on famous writers.

https://albanianstudies.weebly.com/-clothing.html
These photos show the richness of Albanian traditional clothing.

https://theconversation.com/musine-kokalari-a-lost-story-of -defiance-in-the-face-of-political-oppression-83541
The story of Musine Kokalari is told in this 2017 article.

http://whc.unesco.org/en/list/569
This is the World Heritage listing for the Historic Centers of Berat and Gjirokaster.

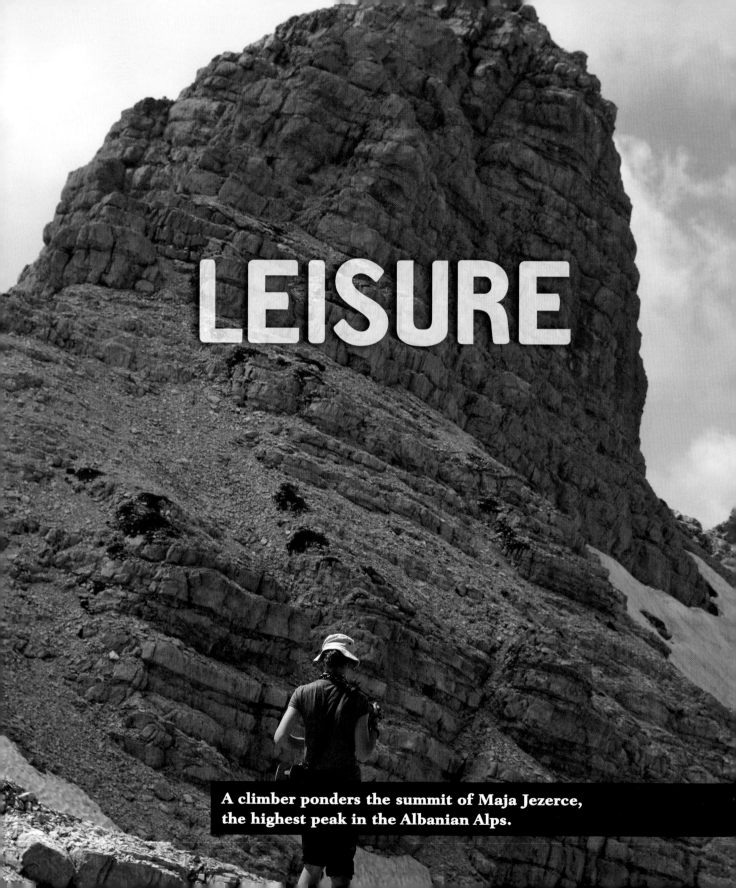

LEISURE

A climber ponders the summit of Maja Jezerce,
the highest peak in the Albanian Alps.

11

LIKE PEOPLE EVERYWHERE, Albanians use much of their spare time to play or watch sports and television shows. With family and friends often scattered far and wide throughout the world, they place a very high value on keeping in touch. An evening stroll, a visit to the house of friends, or a few hours in a coffeehouse are an important part of the day. Today, the internet connects many people with friends and family abroad, and they keep track of each other through email and text messaging.

Shopping and browsing bazaars is a popular leisure activity, particularly in Tirana and other urban areas. Several shopping malls have popped up around the country, often anchored by Italian department stores.

SPORTS

The quality of sports and other organized recreational activities has always been linked to the nation's social, political, and economic situation. Between World War II and the 1990s, though Albania supported sports programs, the nation's lack of economic and social progress resulted in

Children jump into the sea off a floating dock in Sarande, Albania.

levels of play that failed to rival those of the Soviet Union and other European communist nations. Albania's emergence from decades of international isolation has had both rewards and drawbacks for sports fans and athletes.

On the one hand, Albanians have greater variety in the athletic and recreational activities available to them. On the other hand, many Albanians—especially children and young adults—see their freedom as a chance to leave Albania and live, work, and play abroad.

Despite the problems facing schools that cannot afford organized athletic programs, Albanians enjoy many sports and outdoor activities, such as swimming, hiking, and mountain climbing. Albania also fields players and teams in many sports that involve various levels of national and international competition, including basketball, shooting, volleyball, and of course, soccer.

SOCCER

Outside of the United States, soccer is almost universally called football, and it's undeniably Europe's most popular team sport, at both the participatory and spectator levels. This is certainly true in Albania.

The sport was probably introduced to Albania by Christian missionaries in the early 1900s, when Albania was under Ottoman rule. Following World War I, British troops stationed in Albania helped make the game more popular, encouraging Albanians to develop local teams of their own.

Albanian Sokol Cikalleshi (*left*) battles a Hungarian opponent in a friendly soccer match at Puskas Stadium in Budapest.

Albanian soccer teams began playing teams from other nations in the early 1920s and formed their own soccer federation in 1930. From 1930 on, all the major cities and towns had their own teams. World War II resulted in a break from international and national competition, but in the 1944—1945 season, soccer teams once again took to the fields in competition for a national championship. Albania was soon playing national teams from other countries, and in 1946, the country hosted the Balkan Cup tournament for teams from throughout the region.

By 1953, however, Albania had become increasingly closed off due to the policies of its new communist government. Despite becoming a member of the Union of European Football Associations (UEFA) in 1954, from November 1953 until June 1963, the Albanian national team played only two international soccer matches, one in 1957 against the People's Republic of China and one in 1958 against East Germany—both communist nations. Throughout this period, the Albanian government continued to support soccer programs at the state, school, and local levels, and Albanians continued to play soccer—but mostly within their own borders in local leagues and for teams playing in Albanian national competitions. In a few instances, talented Albanian players fled their homeland to play for teams in other nations, notably Italy.

In the 1960s, Albanian soccer reentered the international arena. Its national team appeared in the 1964 Olympics, the 1964 and 1968 European Championship

An aerial view shows a soccer stadium in the city of Korce.

Games, and the 1966 World Cup. In the early 1970s, Albania improved its performance in international competition, and in the 1980s, it entered its first international tournament under the auspices of the prestigious UEFA.

Since the end of communist restrictions on emigration in the early 1990s, Albanians have watched many of their nation's most talented players leave for the chance to play in other countries. They have also had their hopes for the national team's success in Europe—and ultimately the World Cup—raised, lowered, and raised again by a succession of coaches from Italy and Germany.

Meanwhile, Albanians continue to enjoy the sport in their cities and towns. The Albanian Football Federation sponsors league play on several levels, and fans throughout the nation follow their favorite teams in the Football Federation's First Division, a league of between 10 and 14 teams in the major cities that compete against one another for the national championship.

Long considered exclusively a men's sport, soccer in Albania didn't include women until the early years of the 21st century. However, women wanted to play, and after a few years of friendly tournament play, a national team finally formed in 2011. As of 2019, there were 10 women's soccer clubs playing domestically in the country

The men's national team wears uniforms of red and black, after the nation's flag, adorned with the double-headed eagle. It has won no major championships—in fact, it almost never qualifies for major tournaments. In 2016, though, the team delighted its fans by qualifying for the first time for the European Championships after beating Armenia 3—0 for second place in Group I. The achievement caused celebrations across Albania, and the capital city was festooned in red and black, the national colors. At Euro 2016, the team won against Romania but failed to advance any further after that. Nevertheless, Albanian fans were thrilled just to see their team place on the international stage.

BASKETBALL

Although basketball in Albania does not inspire nearly the same passion in its fans as soccer, in the leagues that operate locally and under the auspices of the nation's professional basketball organization, the Basketball Federation of Albania (FSHB), there is no shortage of teams and players to follow. In addition to playing within their own A1 and A2 divisions, the FSHB's teams compete within EuroBasket, a confederation of nearly 200 leagues throughout Europe and western Asia. The Albanian women's national basketball team plays as well.

Founded in 1946, the Albanian Basketball League is one of the oldest continuing basketball leagues in the region of the Balkans. Its teams represent most major cities in Albania. Playing pro ball in Europe has become attractive to players from throughout the world, and in this regard, Albania is very much a part of Europe. A look at the roster of many Albanian Basketball League teams will show that Albanian basketball includes players from throughout the world, not just Albania.

Children play basketball on a colorful new court in Tirana.

TENNIS

In the 1930s, tennis became suddenly popular in Albania as students returning from France, Italy, and other Western European countries brought tennis back with them. Tirana and most other major Albanian cities built public tennis courts, and Albanian players even competed against players from other nations in international events.

In the 1950s, however, the public was banned from playing tennis by Albania's communist government, claiming it was a bourgeois sport that was suited only to privileged members of the upper classes in capitalist countries. Most public courts were neglected and fell into disrepair, and Albanians were not allowed to compete in international events. Still, people who worked for the government were allowed to keep playing tennis, and for their pleasure, some of the courts were kept in good shape.

For years, Albania remained a no-show at international tennis events. In 1985, however, the Albanian Tennis Federation was created. Now, with a national tennis association to promote the sport and create a calendar of regular matches and tournaments, the sport has been brought back to life across the country. In the 1990s, Albania struggled to find the funds to keep its courts in playable condition. In 1996, Albania took a huge step in the development of tennis as a national sport. The Albanian Tennis Federation joined the International Tennis Federation and Tennis Europe, opening the door for Albanians to compete in European and world tournaments.

Since then, tennis has been flourishing in many parts of the country, especially in Tirana, where the Tirana Tennis School developed a relationship with a tennis school in Bari, Italy. In 1999, the schools in Tirana and Bari began an exchange program, with coaches and players sharing their tennis experience with one another and scheduling matches between the two schools.

OUTDOOR ACTIVITIES

Albania's beautiful natural settings have given Albanians a wide range of sporting activities. Like children everywhere, Albanian boys and girls play many outdoor games, including skipping rope, hide-and-seek, tag, and volleyball.

In fact, volleyball is popular enough that people of all ages play the sport indoors, primarily in the major cities. Beach volleyball is also an option along the coast.

Swimming in the Adriatic Sea is a popular summer activity, as are fishing and boating in both the Adriatic and Albania's many inland lakes.

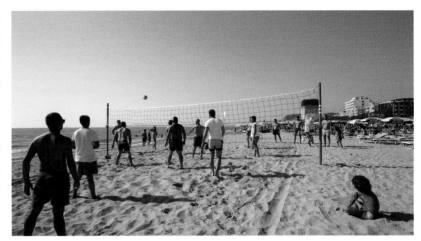

A group of friends enjoy a game of beach volleyball on the sand in Durres.

INTERNET LINKS

https://en.albanianews.it/social/time-young-Albanians
This short article discusses how young people spend their free time in Albania.

https://www.olympic.org/news/news-from-the-albanian-national -olympic-committee
News about the Albanian National Olympic Committee is provided in English on this site.

https://www.uefa.com/memberassociations/association=ALB/ profile/index.html
Information about Albania's national soccer team can be found at this UEFA site.

FESTIVALS

Women in red national dress sing in a
traditional music festival at Berat Castle.

12

LIKE MOST NATIONS, ALBANIA observes a variety of special days throughout the year. Some are religious feast days, some are historical patriotic commemorations, some are secular celebrations, and a few are just oddities that have found their way into the culture.

After several generations of life under atheistic communism, in which religious festivals of all types were banned, Albanians lost the customs they once had. Children grew up with no knowledge or experience of the religion-based holidays that are beloved in much of the world. After freedom arrived, Albanians tried to reclaim those customs, or looked to other countries to copy their traditions. However, the deep-memory associations that make such holidays meaningful will take some time to rebuild. Today, reflecting the religious diversity of the country, there are both Muslim and Christian special days—two of each are national holidays.

The state holidays are the back-to-back Independence Day/Flag Day on November 28 and Liberation Day on November 29. On November 28, 1912, Albania declared its independence from the Ottoman Empire. That same day, Ismail Qemali, the "Founding Father" of modern Albania and principal author of its declaration of independence, raised the double-headed eagle flag that would become the symbol of the new nation. Liberation Day, November 29, is unrelated to the events of the day before. Rather, this day celebrates the country's liberation from Nazi occupation in 1944 during World War II. Following shortly afterward is National Youth

Fireworks sparkle above Tirana in a New Year's display.

Day on December 8, which is a new holiday in honor of Albanian young people's contribution to democracy.

The world's top secular holiday, New Year's Day, is celebrated on January 1 and 2, and the widely celebrated International Labor Day is observed on May 1. Additionally, the day of the elections for the Assembly is a national holiday, whenever it occurs. Though not an official public holiday, Albanian Alphabet Day is considered important nonetheless, especially in the schools. November 22 commemorates the Congress of Manastir, which standardized and adopted the current Albanian alphabet in 1908.

MUSLIM HOLIDAYS

The two most important Muslim holy days are Eid al-Fitr and Eid al-Adha. The dates for these holy days are determined by the Islamic calendar, and therefore they rotate through the seasons, falling on a different date each

Muslim holy days follow the Islamic calendar, which begins counting years from 622 CE, the year the Prophet Muhammad fled from Mecca to Medina, an event called the Hegira. The year 2021, therefore, corresponds to an overlap of the years 1442–1443 AH on the Islamic calendar. The AH means Anno Hegirae *(Latin for "in the year of the Hegira.") It is used in the same way Christians and Westerners use AD* (Anno Domini, *"in the year of the Lord") or, as in this book, CE (Common Era).*

Unlike the 365-day Gregorian, or Western, calendar used internationally—which is based on Earth's orbit around the sun—the Islamic calendar is based on the lunar month, which is only 29 or 30 days long. One Islamic year lasts 354 or 355 days, in a cycle of 12 Islamic months.

Therefore, Islamic festivals don't fall on the same dates of the Western calendar each year. Instead, they rotate by moving forward about 11 days every year. It takes 32.5 years (according to the Western calendar) before a festival once again falls on the same date in the Western calendar. For this reason, Islamic festivals are not associated with any particular time of year, like Christian festivals, but can fall in any season.

Albania uses the Western calendar for nonreligious dates and for some of its Christian holidays.

year. In Albania, they are both national holidays for everyone, regardless of their religion.

The holiest month in the Islamic calendar is Ramadan. It is a time of fasting from sunrise to sundown, a pious undertaking performed in the spirit of prayer and somber introspection. Ramadan is when Muslims focus on their relationship with Allah, or God. When the holy month is over, it's time to feast and celebrate, and that joyous occasion is Eid al-Fitr. Families, friends, and whole communities come together to sing and dance, play traditional music, and feast on foods prepared according to old family recipes. The celebrations continue long into the night, propelled by stories the older generation heard from their parents.

Eid al-Adha, or the Festival of the Sacrifice, may not be as much fun as the other holy day, but it's actually the holier and more important of the two. The day commemorates the story of Ibrahim (the Biblical Abraham), and his willingness to sacrifice his son Ismail (Ishmael) at Allah's command.

Traditions for this somber holy day include prayer; the sacrifice of an animal and a distribution of its meat among family, friends, and the needy; and feasting with the customary foods.

CHRISTIAN HOLIDAYS

Albanian Christians celebrate Christmas with family gatherings and special church services. However, Christmas, called Krishtlindjet, is not as big a festival as New Year's, and Christmas trees have not caught on much, except in tourist areas. Though both Catholics and Orthodox Christians celebrate Christmas, they do so on different days because they follow different religious calendars. In Albania, Catholic Christmas Day, December 25, is recognized as a national holiday, but Orthodox Christmas, which is usually on January 7, is not. (Curiously, both Catholic Easter and Orthodox Easter, which typically occurs the following week, are national holidays, but they both always fall on a Sunday anyway.)

Because December 25 is a national holiday, even non-Christians may have family gatherings on that day. The people of Tirana hold a music festival as well at Christmastime, during which local and international musicians perform traditional and classical music for large crowds.

EASTER

Unlike Christmas, Easter is a movable holiday, though it always falls in the springtime. Easter is the holiest of Christian holidays and is marked by solemn processions to churches in villages and cities throughout the country. Red eggs are important to Albanian Christians at Easter, and people will dye them and tap them gently against their friends's eggs in greeting. In communities where religious differences are not taken too seriously, Muslims and Christians also exchange eggs. Women traditionally dye enough eggs to give to anyone who calls at their house between Maundy Thursday, the day before the crucifixion, and the Ascension, which is celebrated 40 days after Easter.

If a young woman is to be married during the Easter season, her future mother-in-law will give her an egg and a candle at the Easter service. The gift is to assure her fertility.

MOTHER TERESA CANONIZATION DAY

New to the Albanian calendar of festivals is a national holiday on September 5. This day marks the day in 2016 that Anjeze Gonxhe Bojaxhiu, otherwise known as Mother Teresa, was declared a saint by the Roman Catholic Church.

Born in 1910 to ethnic Albanian parents in Skopje, (now the capital of North Macedonia), she took the name Teresa upon joining a religious order as a nun. She performed most of her life's work in the slums of Calcutta (now called Kolkata), India, where she devoted herself to people she called "the poorest of the poor" and founded an order of similarly devoted young women called the Missionaries of Charity. By 1996, Teresa operated 517 such missions in over 100 countries.

Over time, Teresa became known and much beloved around the world (though she also had her detractors). In 1979, she was awarded the Nobel Peace Prize. She died on September 5, 1997, and today she is revered by Catholics as Saint Teresa of Calcutta. Although she was never a citizen of Albania, her ethnic Albanian roots connect her to the country, and her feast day is now celebrated there every year.

A statue of Mother Teresa is displayed at Saint Paul's Catholic Church in Tirana.

FAMILY AND COMMUNITY CELEBRATIONS

Albanians have traditionally had large families and have celebrated family milestones in festive gatherings. Weddings, births, funerals, and birthdays are all cause for people to sing, dance, tell stories, and eat traditional foods

People enjoy Za Fest, an art and music festival in Theth National Park.

prepared as they have been through generations. Dance and music festivals occur throughout the country, especially in the warmer weather, when they can be held outdoors.

DITA E VERES   One of the most popular of those festivals is Dita e Veres, or Summer Day, which has its roots in pagan festivities and Albanian mythology that dates to pre-Roman times. Albania only declared this day a national holiday in 2004, but it's said to be quite ancient. It takes place on March 14, around the time of the spring equinox, and marks the end of winter and the rebirth of nature.

The origin legend of this celebration begins in the ancient city of Elbasan, where Zana, the goddess of flora (plantlife), lived in her mountain temple. She emerged from the temple only once a year, on March 14, which signaled the beginning of summer (in the old days in Europe, there were only two seasons, winter and summer). This legend was passed from generation to generation.

Today, Elbasan hosts the largest of the country's Summer Day festivals, with parades, concerts, bonfires, flowers, and plenty of *ballakume*, a special kind of cookie associated with this day.

NEVRUS Another Albanian national holiday to welcome spring follows closely on the heels of Dita e Veres. Nevrus (also seen as Novruz or Nowruz), means "New Day," and it is often called the Persian New Year. Like Dita e Veres, this day corresponds to the spring equinox and is said to date back around 5,000 years. Albanians celebrate it on March 22. While the holiday might have its roots in Babylonian cultures, Albanian mythology adopted it as its own. Accordingly, it's said to be the day that God created the world, the sun, and human beings.

In the Bektashi communities, Nevrus is Bektashi Order Day, which is probably the main reason why this is a national holiday in Albania. Bektashis use the old Persian New Year to mark the birth of Ali, the son-in-law of the Prophet Muhammad, whom the Bektashi particularly revere. It's also the day to celebrate the wedding of Ali to Fatima, Muhammad's daughter. In addition, the day also marks the Prophet's designation of Ali as his successor. So, for the small Bektashi sect in Albania, Nevrus is an important Muslim holiday.

INTERNET LINKS

https://www.timeanddate.com/holidays/albania
This calendar site lists the holidays and observances in Albania.

https://www.tripsavvy.com/christmas-in-albania-1501183
This travel site describes the Christmas holiday in Albania.

http://www.visit-tirana.com/news/view/170/Albania_has_'two_Easters'_-_here_is_how_we_celebrate_them
The revival of Albanian Easter traditions is the focus of this short article.

FOOD

Fresh produce is offered for sale at
an outdoor market in Kruje.

13

THE CUISINE OF ALBANIA REFLECTS its history and geographical position. A strong Turkish influence came in with the takeover of the Ottomans in the 16th century. This is seen in the flaky pastries such as savory *byrek* and sweet baklava. The influence of Muslim culture also explains the preponderance of lamb in the diet, as pork is forbidden in Islam.

Greek and Italian cuisine also play a large part in traditional Albanian fare, especially the emphasis on olives and olive oil, and the love of oregano, basil, rosemary, and other herbs. The Mediterranean climate of the Adriatic Sea makes it possible to grow figs, olives, grapes, citrus and stone fruits, berries, and most vegetables. Many Albanians have fruit trees in their yards. In the mountainous areas, sheep and cattle graze in the meadows, and the coastal regions offer an abundance of fish and other seafood.

FAVORITE FOODS

Vegetables and fruits in Albania are especially delicious. Favorite vegetables in the summer include eggplant, tomatoes, peppers, cucumbers, green beans, and okra. In the winter, cabbages, carrots, and potatoes, all vegetables that keep well, are used in stews and soups. Electricity limitations in the recent past kept people from freezing food, and poor roads inhibited shipping, so many Albanians eat seasonally and locally.

Albanians are among the world's greatest lovers of onions. The country's rate of onion consumption per capita is often in the top five worldwide.

A man prepares *cevapi* at an outdoor grill in Shkoder.

In the winter, for example, people make salads from pickled vegetables such as cucumbers, peppers, and eggplant.

Traditional Balkan dishes are also much loved in Albania. *Byrek,* or *pite,* for example, is a flaky pie with layers of meat, cheese, or greens. *Qebapa,* or *cevapi,* are grilled sausage-shaped meats made of ground beef and pork; *kofte* are grilled meatballs. These delicious favorites are enjoyed across the Balkan region.

Lamb is Albania's most popular meat. Often, it is roasted on a spit, especially in restaurants, where it is sliced off for use in sandwiches. Economic constraints often mean that Albanians eat as much of the lamb as they can, including the heart, the liver, the brains, the kidneys, and whatever organs there are left. One Albanian specialty is *pace koke* (PAH-seh KOH-keh), a breakfast soup made from the sheep's head.

CAFÉ CULTURE

Albanians love their kafe *(coffee)! This has created a rich café scene in the cities, particularly in Tirana. In fact, Albania became the country with the most cafés per capita in the world in 2016. That doesn't mean Albanians are the top coffee consumers; they're not even in the top 20. (In 2016, the number-one spot went to the Finns.) Rather, Albanians sip their beloved java slowly, from tiny cups—not in their cars, not while walking down the street, but at charming and convivial cafés. Albanians are not ones to order a quick cup of coffee to go.*

From early morning to late in the evening, cafés are full of devoted patrons sipping espresso or Turkish coffee. People take their time with coffee, sitting with friends around a small table. Most coffee shops also have pastries, cookies, cakes, or croissants. In Tirana, many cafés offer cappuccinos, lattes, smoothies, milkshakes, and fresh juices as well.

Turli perimesh, or Albanian vegetables, is a light vegetable stew, similar to a French ratatouille.

Tave kosi is one of Albania's national dishes. The casserole of baked lamb, rice, and yogurt is a specialty of Elbasan, a city near Tirana, but the dish is much beloved across the entire country.

TYPICAL MEALS

Albanian cooks find ways to stretch their food, especially meat. Chopped meat provides the protein in many meals, stuffed into cabbage leaves, peppers, potatoes, and zucchini. Yogurt and cheese are also used to make meat go further. One dish, *turli* (TOOR-lih), layers any vegetable the cook has available with tomatoes and simmers them all with a cut of veal to serve the whole family. In Albania, veal is the meat of a calf that is allowed to grow for a longer time, and to a larger size, to produce more meat than in most other countries.

A main meal on Sunday or for guests might typically include an appetizer or salad, a main meal, and a dessert and coffee. Most of what Albanians eat will be what is locally available because shipping throughout the country adds so much to the cost. The first course might consist of tomatoes, either with or without vinegar, and a chewy bread that is dipped in warm, thick yogurt. The main meal could be chicken, beef, mutton, or fish. Along the Adriatic or Ionian coasts, there is a wide variety of fish, but inland, it is most likely to be carp, a fish that feeds on the bottom of the river. Noodles accompany many entrées.

Dessert is often fruit, such as figs or prunes, or crème caramel, an egg custard topped with caramelized sugar.

DRINKS

Beverages include bottled or boiled water, Turkish coffee, wine, and raki, the Albanian brandy. There is also Italian beer, as well as beers made by local breweries.

Albania has a very old wine-making tradition, and its wines today are very popular. Grapes grow well in the mountainous north of the country. The highest vineyards are found at altitudes of 3,300 to 4,300 feet (1,000 to 1,300 m), on the slopes of the Albanian Alps. However, lowland and coastal regions also do well with certain kinds of grapes.

The traditional alcoholic drink is raki. This clear liquor is usually made from grapes, although Albanians also make it from mulberries or plums. It is most often enjoyed by men in the morning, but it is also considered a digestive aid and can be consumed just about any time at all.

Most commonly, the drink of choice is coffee, traditionally *kafe turke* (KAH-feh TURK), or Turkish coffee. In Albanian homes in the villages and countryside, kafe turke is what will be served to guests. It is made by combining finely ground coffee, water, and sugar in one pot and boiling it until it is ready. Served in small cups, kafe turke helps provide the proper atmosphere for arranging marriages, making deals, and resolving disagreements short of a blood feud. In the cities, coffee is most often prepared in Italian espresso machines.

INTERNET LINKS

https://www.myalbanianfood.com
This home cookery site includes many recipes with commentary.

https://www.thecrazytourist.com/traditional-food-albania
This post provides a quick overview of essential Albanian dishes.

TAVE KOSI (ALBANIAN BAKED LAMB AND YOGURT)

6 tablespoons butter, divided
1 tablespoon olive oil
2 pounds (900 grams) lamb shoulder or leg,
   trimmed and cut into bite-sized pieces
Salt and pepper, to taste
⅓ cup white rice
4 cloves garlic, minced
1 cup water
3 tablespoons finely chopped fresh oregano
   (or 1 tablespoon dried)
2 tablespoons flour
4 cups plain Greek-style yogurt
⅛ teaspoon nutmeg
5 eggs
Chopped fresh herbs for garnish

Heat the oven to 375°F (190°C). Heat 3 tablespoons butter and the oil in a large frying pan over medium-high heat. Season the lamb with salt and pepper. Working in batches, brown the lamb, turning occasionally, about 10—12 minutes. Place all of the browned meat back in the pan. Add the rice and garlic; stir. Add water; bring to a boil. Cover pan, and reduce heat to medium-low; cook until rice is just tender, about 18 minutes. Stir in oregano, plus more salt and pepper, and transfer to a 9 x 13-inch (23 x 33-centimeter) baking dish; set aside.

Melt the remaining 3 tablespoons butter in a medium saucepan over medium-high heat. Whisk in the flour; cook the roux until smooth, about 2 minutes, but don't let it brown. Remove from the heat; whisk in the yogurt, nutmeg, eggs, salt, and pepper until smooth. Pour the yogurt sauce evenly over the lamb mixture in the baking dish.

Bake uncovered until golden and puffed, 45—60 minutes. Sprinkle with fresh chopped herbs, such as parsley or mint. Serves 8—10.

SHENDETLIE (ALBANIAN WALNUT CAKE)

1½ cups sugar
3 eggs
¾ cup melted butter, cooled
5½ cups flour
3 ounces (85 grams) walnuts, finely chopped
4 tablespoons honey
1 teaspoon baking soda

For the syrup:
1 cup sugar
1¾ cups water

Preheat the oven to 350°F (175°C).

(Note: A stand mixer with a paddle beater is recommended for this firm dough.)

In a large bowl, beat the eggs, sugar, and melted butter together. Add honey and baking soda. Add half of the flour and all of the walnuts, and mix well. Add the rest of the flour, and mix until the dough is smooth and firm.

Line a 12-inch (30.5 cm) cake pan with parchment paper. Using wet hands, press the dough evenly into the pan.

Bake for 35—40 minutes, or until the dough has turned dark brown and is firm to the touch.

Remove from the oven, and let the cake cool completely.

Meanwhile, prepare the syrup. Pour the sugar and water into a medium saucepan, and bring to a boil. Reduce heat to medium-low, and boil for 15 minutes, stirring occasionally. Remove the pan from the heat.

Cut the cooled cake into diamond shapes, but do not remove from the pan. Pour the hot syrup over the cake, completely covering it. Refrigerate for at least 2 hours before serving.

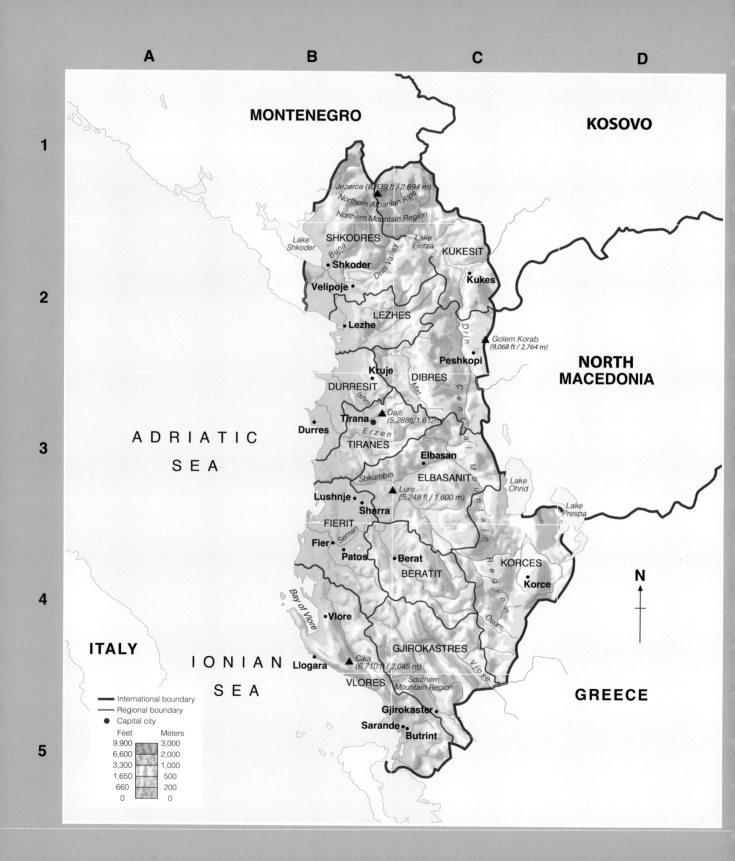

A B C D

MONTENEGRO   KOSOVO

1

Jezerce (8,839 ft / 2,694 m)
Northern Albanian Alps
Northern Mountain Region

SHKODRES   *Lake*
Lake   *Fierza*
Shkoder   KUKESIT
• **Shkoder**
Velipoje •   **Kukes** •

2

LEZHES
Lezhe •
                                        Golem Korab
                                        (9,068 ft / 2,764 m)
                                Peshkopi •

Kruje •   DIBRES   NORTH
DURRESIT   MACEDONIA
                   ▲ *Dajti*
Tirana •   *(5,288ft/1,612m)*
Durres •   *Erzen*
A D R I A T I C   TIRANES

3

S E A   **Elbasan** •
                   ELBASANIT
                   Shkumbin   *Lake*
                                           Ohrid
                   ▲ *Lure*
Lushnje •   *(5,248 ft / 1,600 m)* *Lake*
Sharra •   *Prespa*
FIERIT
Seman
Fier •   KORCES
Patos •   **Berat** •
                   BERATIT   **Korce** •

4   N

Vlore •
Bay of Vlore   *Osum*
                   GJIROKASTRES
I O N I A N   ▲ *Cika*
Llogara •   *(6,710 ft / 2,045 m)*
S E A   VLORES   *Southern*
ITALY   *Mountain Region*   GREECE

Gjirokaster •
Sarande •
Butrint

5

—— International boundary
—— Regional boundary
• Capital city

Feet   Meters
9,900   3,000
6,600   2,000
3,300   1,000
1,650   500
660   200
0   0

MAP OF ALBANIA

ECONOMIC ALBANIA

Services

 Airport

 Port

 Tourism

Natural Resources

 Chrome

 Copper

 Fish

 Oil

 Steel

Manufacturing

 Food processing

 Machinery and building materials

 Textiles

 Wood and timber

Agriculture

 Cotton

Sugar beets

Tobacco

ABOUT THE ECONOMY

All figures are 2017 estimates unless otherwise noted.

NATURAL RESOURCES
petroleum, natural gas, coal, bauxite, chromite, copper, iron ore, nickel, salt, timber, hydropower

GDP (OFFICIAL EXCHANGE RATE)
$13.07 billion

GDP PER CAPITA
$12,500

GDP BY SECTOR OF ORIGIN
agriculture: 21.7 percent
industry: 24.2 percent
services: 54.1 percent

LABOR FORCE
1.198 million

LABOR FORCE BY OCCUPATION
agriculture: 41.4 percent
industry: 18.3 percent
services: 40.3 percent

POPULATION BELOW POVERTY LINE
14.3 percent

INDUSTRIAL PRODUCTS
food processing, textiles and clothing, lumber, oil, cement, chemicals, mining, basic metals, hydropower

AGRICULTURAL PRODUCTS
wheat, corn, potatoes, vegetables, fruits, olives and olive oil, grapes; meat and dairy products; sheep and goats

MAJOR EXPORTS
textiles and footwear, asphalt, metals and metallic ores, crude oil, vegetables, fruits, tobacco

EXPORT PARTNERS
Italy, Kosovo, Spain, Greece

MAJOR IMPORTS
machinery and equipment, foodstuffs, textiles, chemicals

IMPORT PARTNERS
Italy, Turkey, Germany, Greece, China, Serbia

UNEMPLOYMENT RATE
13.8 percent

CURRENCY
Albanian lek (ALL; plural leke)
1.00 USD = 110.27 ALL (January 2020)
notes: 200, 500, 1,000, 2,000, 5,000, 10,000 leke
coins: 1, 5, 10, 20, 50, 100 leke

CULTURAL ALBANIA

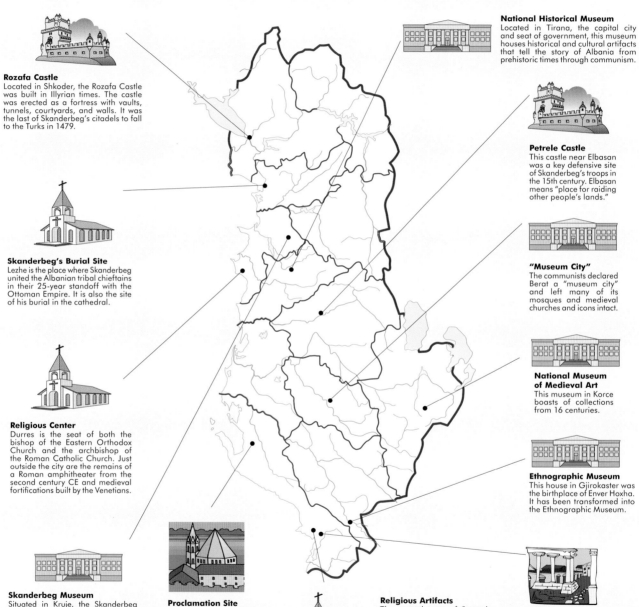

Rozafa Castle
Located in Shkoder, the Rozafa Castle was built in Illyrian times. The castle was erected as a fortress with vaults, tunnels, courtyards, and walls. It was the last of Skanderbeg's citadels to fall to the Turks in 1479.

Skanderbeg's Burial Site
Lezhe is the place where Skanderbeg united the Albanian tribal chieftains in their 25-year standoff with the Ottoman Empire. It is also the site of his burial in the cathedral.

Religious Center
Durres is the seat of both the bishop of the Eastern Orthodox Church and the archbishop of the Roman Catholic Church. Just outside the city are the remains of a Roman amphitheater from the second century CE and medieval fortifications built by the Venetians.

Skanderbeg Museum
Situated in Kruje, the Skanderbeg Museum was initially the ancestral home of Albania's national hero. It was the center of the Albanian resistance during the Ottoman invasion.

Proclamation Site
Vlore is the place where the Adriatic and Ionian Seas divide. The city is also the site where Albanian independence was proclaimed in 1912.

Religious Artifacts
The coastal town of Sarande has yielded the remains of a Christian basilica dating to the fifth and sixth centuries CE, multicolored mosaics, and a Christian monastery. Sarande is now part of the Albanian Riviera.

National Historical Museum
Located in Tirana, the capital city and seat of government, this museum houses historical and cultural artifacts that tell the story of Albania from prehistoric times through communism.

Petrele Castle
This castle near Elbasan was a key defensive site of Skanderbeg's troops in the 15th century. Elbasan means "place for raiding other people's lands."

"Museum City"
The communists declared Berat a "museum city" and left many of its mosques and medieval churches and icons intact.

National Museum of Medieval Art
This museum in Korce boasts of collections from 16 centuries.

Ethnographic Museum
This house in Gjirokaster was the birthplace of Enver Hoxha. It has been transformed into the Ethnographic Museum.

Roman Ruins
Butrint was the site of an ancient urban center. Its ruins include a theater, Roman baths, and other archaeological riches.

ABOUT THE CULTURE

All figures are 2020 estimates unless otherwise noted.

OFFICIAL COUNTRY NAME
Republika e Shqiperise
short form: Shqiperia
English: Republic of Albania

GOVERNMENT TYPE
parliamentary republic

FLAG DESCRIPTION
a black, two-headed eagle in the center, with a red background

CAPITAL
Tirana

ADMINISTRATIVE DIVISIONS
12 counties (*qarqe*; singular, *qark*):
Beratit, Dibres, Durresit, Elbasanit, Fierit, Gjirokastres, Korces, Kukesit, Lezhes, Shkodres, Tiranes, Vlores

POPULATION
3,074,579

ETHNIC GROUPS
Albanian 82.6 percent, Greek 0.9 percent, other 1 percent (including Vlach, Roma, Macedonian, Montenegrin, and Egyptian), unspecified 15.5 percent (2011)

RELIGIONS
Muslim 56.7 percent, Roman Catholic 10 percent, Orthodox 6.8 percent, atheist 2.5 percent, Bektashi (a Sufi order) 2.1 percent, other 5.7 percent, unspecified 16.2 percent (2011)

LANGUAGES
Albanian 98.8 percent (official, derived from Tosk dialect), Greek 0.5 percent, other 0.6 percent (including Macedonian, Romani, Vlach, Turkish, Italian, and Serbo-Croatian), unspecified 0.1 percent (2011)

POPULATION GROWTH RATE
0.28 percent

NET MIGRATION RATE
-3.3 migrants per 1,000 population

URBANIZATION
62.1 percent

LIFE EXPECTANCY AT BIRTH
total population: 79 years
male: 76.3 years
female: 81.9 years

LITERACY RATE
98.1 percent

TIMELINE

IN ALBANIA	IN THE WORLD
400–300 BCE The Illyrian kingdom reaches its peak of power.	**334–323 BCE** Alexander the Great creates an empire stretching from Greece to Afghanistan.
165 BCE Rome captures Albania.	
732 CE Illyrian lands come under rule of Constantinople.	
1389 Ottomans take over some Albanian lands.	**1054** The Great Schism divides Christianity into the Roman Catholic and Eastern Orthodox Churches.
1443 Skanderbeg mounts resistance to the Turks.	
1479 Ottoman rule becomes complete; it will last for 400 years.	
1600–1800 Albania becomes a Muslim land as two-thirds of the people convert to Islam.	**1530** The transatlantic slave trade begins, organized by the Portuguese in Africa.
	1776 The US Declaration of Independence is signed.
	1789–1799 The French Revolution occurs.
1912 Albanians declare Albania independent.	**1914–1918** World War I is fought.
1928 Albania becomes a kingdom under King Zog.	
	1939 World War II begins.
1940 Italy annexes Albania.	
1941 Enver Hoxha founds the Albanian Communist Party.	
1944 Albania forms a communist government; Hoxha is head of state.	**1945** World War II ends.
	1969 US astronaut Neil Armstrong becomes the first human on the moon.
1985 Hoxha dies. He is succeeded by Ramiz Alia, who continues Hoxha's policies and practices.	**1986** A nuclear power disaster occurs at Chernobyl, Ukraine.

IN ALBANIA		IN THE WORLD
1990		
Demonstrations result in a liberalization of the government.		
1991		**1991**
Multiparty elections are held for the first time in 50 years. Albania's old constitution is thrown out.		The Soviet Union breaks up.
1997		**1997**
A government-led pyramid scheme collapses. The Albanian people riot.		Britain returns Hong Kong to China.
1999		
Refugees from Kosovo flee to Albania.		**2001**
		Al-Qaeda terrorists stage the 9/11 attacks in the United States.
2007		
President George W. Bush becomes the first US leader to visit Albania.		**2008**
		The United States elects its first African American president, Barack Obama.
2009		**2009**
Albania joins NATO.		An outbreak of H1N1 flu spreads around the world.
2011		
Anti-corruption demonstrations leave four protesters dead in Tirana.		
2013		
Edi Rama becomes prime minister.		
2014		
Albania becomes a candidate for EU membership. Pope Francis visits Albania.		**2015–2016**
		ISIS launches terror attacks in Belgium and France.
2016		**2016**
The government begins sweeping judicial reforms.		The Catholic Church declares Mother Teresa a saint.
		2017
		Donald Trump becomes the US president.
		2018
		The Winter Olympics are held in South Korea.
2019		**2019**
A strong earthquake kills 51 people and injures 3,000 in northwestern Albania.		Notre Dame Cathedral in Paris is damaged by fire. Donald Trump is impeached.
2020		**2020**
Albania sets earthquake repair estimate at $1.17 billion.		The COVID-19 pandemic spreads around the world.

GLOSSARY

baklava
A sweet dessert made with a filling of ground nuts soaked in honey or sugar syrup, sandwiched between layers of phyllo dough.

besa (BEH-sah)
An Albanian's word of honor, strongly held even to the point of blood feud.

byrek
A pie made from phyllo dough and various stuffings, such as spinach, cheese, and lamb.

Eid al-Fitr
The Muslim celebration of the end of Ramadan; a time of feasting, music, and gathering of friends and family.

ethnic cleansing
A process in which one ethnic group expels, imprisons, or kills civilians of another ethnic group, usually a minority.

Gheg (or Geg)
The people of northern Albania.

gjakmarrja
An Albanian blood feud based on revenge for the sake of honor.

kafe turke (KAH-feh TURK)
Turkish coffee; a strong drink made from boiled water, coffee, and sugar.

Kalashnikov
A Soviet assault rifle capable of firing many bullets with one pull of the trigger.

lahuta
An Albanian stringed instrument, similar to the lute.

pace koke (PAH-seh KOH-keh)
A breakfast soup made from the meat of a sheep's head.

pasha
A local ruling representative of the Ottoman Empire.

pyramid scheme
A fraudulent get-rich-quick plan whereby a few early investors at the top of the pyramid take the money of many later investors at the bottom of the pyramid, who lose everything.

raki
An alcoholic drink, similar to brandy, made and served in Albanian homes as well as commercially.

Shqip (SHKEEP)
The Albanian language. It is unrelated to any other known language and is spoken by Albanians all over the world.

Tosk
Albanians from southern Albania.

FOR FURTHER INFORMATION

BOOKS

Abrahams, Fred C. *Modern Albania*. New York, NY: NYU Press, 2016.

Fevziu, Blendi, and Robert Elsie. *Enver Hoxha: The Iron Fist of Albania.* London, UK: I. B. Tauris, 2017.

Gloyer, Gillian. *Albania*. Chalfont St. Peter, UK: Bradt Travel Guides, 2018.

ONLINE

BalkanInsight. "Albania." https://balkaninsight.com/albania-home.

BBC News. "Albania Country Profile." https://www.bbc.com/news/world-europe-17679574.

BBC News. "Albania Profile: Timeline." https://www.bbc.com/news/world-europe-17681099.

CIA. *The World Factbook*. "Albania." https://www.cia.gov/library/publications/the-world-factbook/geos/al.html.

The Culture Trip. "Albania." https://theculturetrip.com/europe/albania.

Institute of Statistics (INSTAT). http://www.instat.gov.al/en.

MUSIC

Kurbeti: Music of Albania's Gypsies. FM Records, 2011.

Tirana Ensemble. *Polyphonic Chants from Albania*, Iris, 1998.

Tirana Folk Ensemble. *Songs and Dances from Albania*, Arc Music, 2000.

UNESCO Anthology of World Music: Music from Albania. Rounder Select, 1998.

Vocal Traditions of Albania. Saydisc, 2000.

FILM

Dear Albania. American Public Television, 2015.

Wild Albania. Magellan TV, 2016.

BIBLIOGRAPHY

Albanian National Center of Cinematography. "A Short History of Albanian Cinema." https://nationalfilmcenter.wordpress.com/a-short-history-of-albanian-cinema.

Bank of Albania. "Remittances: A Support for Development." June 16, 2018. https://www.bankofalbania.org/rc/doc/Remitancat_Revista_eng_12103.pdf.

CIA. *The World Factbook*. "Albania." https://www.cia.gov/library/publications/the-world-factbook/geos/al.html.

Daraghi, Borozou. "'Colombia of Europe': How Tiny Albania Became the Continent's Drug Trafficking Headquarters." *Independent*, January 27, 2019. https://www.independent.co.uk/news/world/europe/albania-drug-cannabis-trafficking-hub-europe-adriatic-sea-a8747036.html.

Freedom House. "Freedom in the World 2019: Albania." https://freedomhouse.org/report/freedom-world/2019/albania.

GAN Integrity. "Albania Corruption Report." https://www.ganintegrity.com/portal/country-profiles/albania.

Lonely Planet. "Albania." https://www.lonelyplanet.com/albania.

Lukic, Filip. "Vetting Process in Albania—the Marching Failure." European Western Balkans, November 13, 2019. https://europeanwesternbalkans.com/2019/11/13/vetting-process-in-albania-the-marching-failure.

Petrusich, Amanda. "In the Land of Vendettas That Go On Forever." *VQR*, Fall 2017. https://www.vqronline.org/reporting-articles/2017/10/land-vendettas-go-forever?src=longreads.

Pressly, Linda. "Europe's Outdoor Cannabis Capital." BBC News, December 1, 2016. https://www.bbc.com/news/magazine-38111945.

Ramsar Convention. "Albania." https://www.ramsar.org/wetland/albania.

Reed, Monty. "The Inside Story of Europe's First Narco-State." *Vice*, January 6, 2019. https://www.vice.com/en_us/article/zmpq89/the-inside-story-of-europes-first-narco-state.

Sinoruka, Fjori. "Tradition Denies Albanian Women Right to Property." *Balkan Insight*, September 3, 2019. https://balkaninsight.com/2019/09/03/tradition-denies-albanian-women-right-to-property.

Transparency International. "Corruptions Perceptions Index 2019." https://www.transparency.org/cpi2019?/news/feature/cpi-2019.

UNESCO World Heritage Convention. "Albania." https://whc.unesco.org/en/statesparties/al.

Walker, Shaun. "Edi Rama, Albania's Unconventional PM Who Wants to Escape the 'Curse of History.'" *Guardian*, June 10, 2019. https://www.theguardian.com/world/2019/jun/10/edi-rama-albania-pm-escape-curse-of-history.

INDEX

INDEX